PRENTICE-HALL, INC.,
Englewood Cliffs, New Jersey 07632

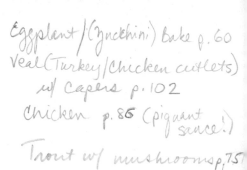

A SPECTRUM BOOK

Eggplant / (Zucchini) Bake p. 60
Veal (Turkey/Chicken cutlets)
w/ capers p. 102
Chicken p. 86 (piquant sauce!)
Trout w/ mushrooms p. 75

MARINA POLVAY

Slim and Healthy Italian Cooking

CUCINA MAGRA, CUCINA SANA

Library of Congress Cataloging in Publication Data

POLVAY, MARINA.
  Cucina magra, cucina sana.

  (The Creative Cooking Series) (A Spectrum Book)
  Text in English.
  Includes index.
  1. Cookery, Italian.   2. Low-calorie diet—Recipes.
I. Title. II. Series: Creative cooking series.
TX723.P64   641.5′635   80-26880
ISBN   0-13-195081-9
ISBN   0-13-195073-8 (pbk.)

Editorial/production supervision by Maria Carella
    and Louise M. Marcewicz
Illustrated by Joan Croom
Art Director: Jeannette Jacobs
Cover design by Honi Werner
Manufacturing buyer: Cathie Lenard

This Spectrum Book can be made available
to businesses and organizations at a special discount
when ordered in large quantities. For more
information, contact:

> Prentice-Hall, Inc.
> General Book Marketing
> Special Sales Division
> Englewood Cliffs, New Jersey 07632

PRENTICE-HALL INTERNATIONAL, INC., *London*
PRENTICE-HALL OF AUSTRALIA PTY. LIMITED, *Sydney*
PRENTICE-HALL OF CANADA, LTD., *Toronto*
PRENTICE-HALL OF INDIA PRIVATE LIMITED, *New Delhi*
PRENTICE-HALL OF JAPAN, INC., *Tokyo*
PRENTICE-HALL OF SOUTHEAST ASIA PTE. LTD., *Singapore*
WHITEHALL BOOKS LIMITED, *Wellington, New Zealand*

CONTENTS

(Pollame)
POULTRY, *83*

(Carne)
MEATS, *93*

(Salse)
SAUCES, *107*

(Pasta e Risotti)
PASTA
AND RICE, *119*

(Dolci)
DESSERTS, *139*

PREFACE

It may seem a bit incongruous for a Russian to write an Italian cookbook, but Italy is one of my favorite countries, where for many years I spent parts of my summer and winter vacations. These were divided among Merano, San Remo, the Lido, Florence, Bari, Capri, or skiing in winter at Cortina.

A few of my relatives, also Russian emigrés, settled in Merano, the former Austrian Imperial resort, and that's where I was first exposed to the intense honesty of fine Italian cooking.

One of my uncles employed a rotund, lively Italian cook, Mamma Contonetti, who had the ability to combine simplicity with culinary elegance. Her cooking was *casalinga*—homey, friendly, and delicious, but her finished dishes were presented in a most artistic and elegant manner.

From my earliest years, one way or another, I wound up in the kitchen—sometimes treated as an unwelcome nuisance, but in the case of Mamma Contonetti, as an eager pupil. From her I learned the best of Tuscan and Northern Italian cooking. Quite soon she allowed me to pinch together ravioli and tortellini, to stir the delicate white sauce, and to puree the fresh, fragrant tomatoes. Rice was usually baked by Mamma "C," and *manicotti* were encased, instead of in the customary pasta, into the thinnest of crepes. Many of her dishes did not have formal names, she just referred to them as "stuffed mushrooms" or "poached fish" or "flaming peaches." At that time my knowledge of Italian culinary terms left much to be desired, and to this day I have not learned the correct Italian names for many of Mamma's dishes. We communicated in my broken Italian, and in her particular brand of southern Tyrolian-Austrian dialect, but there was never a problem or misunderstanding between us. She gave me a love of Italian cuisine and also taught me many refinements. She was quite a storyteller and during our sojourns in the kitchen, plied me with tales of her relatives from Napoli and Calabria who, according to her, practiced one type of cookery only, *"molto pomidori e aglio"*—lots of tomatoes and garlic. For emphasis she would repeat in her Tyrolian dialect "viel Tomate und Knoblauch."

In years to come when I traveled through Italy, or stayed with friends or relatives, I would ask for recipes or how a particular dish was prepared. As my culinary horizons expanded, I became bolder and would ask restaurant managers, maître d's, and chefs for their secrets; and, whenever I could, I would observe a chef creating one of his delicacies. As my Italian improved, so did my culinary repertoire.

I realized that each region, province, and even town and city, in Italy has its own flavor and its own specialties. The robust cooking of the south at which Mamma "C" scoffed vociferously, has a romance and charm of its own; and it is filled with marvelous, tasty, hearty creations. I also found out that the pastries in Sicily, for instance, may just be the best in Italy.

In the last few years when traveling through the boot-shaped *bel passe,* I heard rumblings about a new type of cookery that was invading this bastion of "*la dolce vita.*" Italians were becoming figure and diet conscious. The younger generation, especially, was spearheading a culinary revolution by using less butter, cream, cheese, and oil, by eating a minimum amount of sweets, and by reducing portions. At first, the traditionalists frowned at the very idea of changing beloved recipes. But then at the insistence of their physicians, or perhaps out of sheer vanity, they began their own experimentations with the new *cucina sana;* the restaurants were not far behind.

With my curiosity piqued, I spent time at Montecatini's Grand Hotel and La Pace spa that is reputed to be the cradle of *cucina sana,* and obtained quite an education on the principles of this new approach.

I also asked friends who, if not practitioners of the new cooking technique, inevitably knew someone who was an exponent of *"magra"* (*"sana"*). This gave me an opportunity to observe a wide variety of devotees who initiated me into the intricacies of "slim cookery." After working with several cooks employed by my friends, plus a coterie of restaurant chefs, as well as amateur chefs who did not have help in the kitchen, I have gained an excellent insight into this welcome addition to Italian gastronomy. I feel that anyone who tries the new recipes will be rewarded with *Buona sana*—good health!

To my friend and mentor, Mamma Cantonetti, who instilled in me a love for Italian cooking and gave me some of her treasured recipes.

To scores of my Italian friends, who let me putter in their kitchens and introduced me to the changing eating habits in Italy and *cucina magra.*

As always to Joan Mittelman, my right hand and editor.

To Wescott Devine, who deciphered all the illegible recipes and other scribbles.

To Marise Pokorny, who finally made me write my first Italian cookbook.

Marina Polvay
Miami Shores, Florida

INTRODUCTION

The common denominator of Italian cooking has always been love and caring, simplicity, fresh ingredients, and the creativity of the cook. Italian cuisine, in greater part, is the creation of Italian housewives. Far from being confined to the heavy, spicy, tomato-laden gastronomy we have become accustomed to in this country, Italian cooking, in actuality, is dominated by dishes delicately flavored with unique combinations of herbs and spices. It is also true that butter, oil, cream, and cheeses are often used profusely, resulting in delectable, but quite fattening dishes.

After the lean years of World War II, a wave of overindulgence swept Italy, bringing with it new health hazards. This was a time when butter, cream, cheeses, and sugar were really dished out with a heavy hand. For years physicians warned their patients against "too much of everything," but Italians are gastronomes and accepting the concept of a new diet was contrary to their basic instincts.

Italian gourmands were used to overindulging all year long and then taking their corpulent bodies to one of the health spas for a "cure." They believed that their bodies would be cleansed of all impurities, their stomachs revitalized, and their circulation improved during a 2-to-3 week stay. They shed a few pounds by dieting, drinking vile tasting purgative waters, taking baths, steam, massage, and health walks, and returned home feeling rejuvenated, restored and ready for another year of overindulgence.

It took quite some time for eating habits to be re-formed and new cooking techniques devised. Once this occurred, the artistic nature of the Italians took over and home cooks and chefs alike began formulating new recipes to achieve exciting nuances and subtleties of taste and texture.

Cucina magra or *cucina sana,* the slimming or healthful cuisine, is outstanding in its simplicity and elegance. It has been gathering momentum and has invaded the domain of *cucina casalinga,* the substantial home cooking, which is slowly giving way.

In general, Italian cuisine does not follow rigid culinary dictates devised by pompous epicureans. It does not depend on elaborate and complicated preparation techniques for its success. The only requisites are that the ingredients be fresh and that the finished product be a joy to consume.

The cuisine of Italy is unpretentious and relatively simple to prepare. It is also ruggedly individualistic and, like the Italians themselves, charming and captivating. All these qualities are an integral part of *cucina magra* which gained its foundation and refinements from many regional sources unlike the highly touted *cusine minceur.*

The concept of *cuisine minceur,* the French lighter, lo-cal cooking, is to exercise all the intricacies and techniques of classic *haute cuisine,* but without so many calories. Adherence to old-time techniques makes *cuisine minceur* quite involved. It requires dedication, a great deal of time, and a good basic knowledge of French cooking techniques.

On the contrary, *cucina magra,* being a much more simple culinary endeavor, is easier to follow and leaves room for the individual cook's imagination, creativity, and shortcuts. Have your pasta, rice, or *polenta,* but use very little butter, oil, or cream—and try cheeses with less fat content. Steam vegetables and serve them with a vinaigrette. Reduce oil and butter to a minimum in all dishes and consider deep frying a malfeasance. You don't have to be a master chef with a great deal of expertise or someone who knows all the "trucs" of *la grande cuisine,* to cook healthier, less fattening, tasty dishes, and to be as creative as you please.

Historically, Italian gastronomy came from the four corners of the world. As early as the first century A.D., food and delicacies were brought to Rome from its widespread colonies: wheat from Egypt, olive oil from Spain, rare spices from Asia, and exotic fruit from Judea.

The cuisine of Italy is a mélange of culinary achievements from as far away as Cathay and the New World. Even today each province and hamlet, from the towering, snow-capped Alps to the parched tip of the boot, has its own flavor and cooking techniques.

Venetia's cooking emphasizes spicy sauces, crisp vegetables, and seafood prepared with a great deal of sophistication, lending itself easily to *cucina magra.*

Bologna and Parma are considered fine food capitals of Italy. Salami, hams, smoked meats, and Parmesan cheese originated here, along with the Bolognese *ragù:* rich meat, cream, and butter sauce.

Lombardy's cooking is more delicate and aromatic, with superb smoked meats and dairy products. Many dishes are flavored with saffron, and rice is used more often than pasta, chiefly because rice grows so abundantly in the Po Valley just to the south.

Liguria, which stretches west and southeast from Genoa, is famous for its inimitable *pesto,* a basil-based sauce; its *burrida,* a spicy fish soup; and its small fried fish known as *bianchetti fritti.*

Tuscany and Florence have their own *haute cuisine:* here the butter-oriented cookery of the North undergoes a subtle change with the addition of a fine olive oil. Specialties are centered around spinach, which has been recognized since Roman times as having health-giving qualities. The meats are grilled over open fires, and vegetables, and fruit are an integral part of the cuisine. *Cucina magra* is a natural in this area.

Roman cooking conjures visions of Lucullan feasts that have become legend, but today, the main aspect of Roman dining is *ambiente* (atmosphere).

South of Rome, in Abruzzi, Campania, Apulia, and Calabria, pasta of all shapes with pungent tomato sauce dominates the cuisine. Naples is the center of culinary achievement in the South and is the real home of pasta and pizza.

Sicilian cookery is as robust as its people and consists of many aromatic sauces served over macaroni and meats. Seafood is varied, and the desserts are among the best in Italy.

These cities and regions have remained individualistic in their approaches, even when altering or modifying their cooking styles to suit *cucina magra* principles.

Cucina magra has gained popularity at the grass-roots level—among home cooks. In addition to avoiding rich sauces, pastas saturated with butter, and heavy desserts, they cook vegetables, fruit, fish, and meat only until their natural flavors emerge, and serve them in their own juices.

"Less is best" has become the philosophy for discriminating, health conscious diners. Thus, *cucina magra* also has appeared quietly on restaurant menus in Florence, Milano, and Rome and has become part of the culinary repertoire.

Some of the most sophisticated and painstaking *cucina magra* dishes are prepared in the health spas which are scattered throughout Italy. One such resort, the Natural Health Spa and Grand Hotel in Montecatini, nestled among the hills of Tuscany about 20 miles from Florence, claims to be the forerunner in the art of healthful Italian cooking.

The fruits and vegetables used at this spa, and for that matter throughout most of Tuscany, are cultivated in the rich Tuscan soil, without chemicals.

Vegetable fields are just a few kilometers away and the farmers pick out tiny tender zucchini, spotless green spinach, and tomatoes, daily. Partially ripe tomatoes are considered better for salads, and are said to be healthier than the luscious, red, ripe ones. The branches of fruit trees—peaches, apricots, figs, and plums—are weighted down with their succulent fruits and melons ripen in the bright sunlight, adding their marvelous perfume to the mixture of pungent, natural scents.

Among the trees, patches of strawberries and bushes of raspberries and blackberries grow in profusion. Nearby grow the delicate small wild strawberries which are a favorite with fresh milk for breakfast and dessert.

The eggs and poultry also come from local farms and the whole-wheat bread is baked at country bakeries.

In many parts of today's Italy, especially in the countryside, meat is served sparsely. In the coastal regions fish and seafood predominate and are prepared with great flair and imagination.

Pasta is certainly a staple on the menu across the land. Contrary to popular belief pasta, properly cooked and served, is not a pound builder, but a welcome addition to a well-balanced, healthy diet.

Pasta in itself is low in fat, contains energy-giving carbohydrates (more so than potatoes) and also, protein.

Supplemented with marvelous light sauces, it can be converted into a nutritionally nearly perfect food. Just add fresh vegetables, cheese, eggs, fruit (tomatoes actually are fruit), and presto—there is your balanced diet with plenty of protein and with all the essential amino acids intact.

Exponents of *cucina sana* try as often as possible to grill their meat, fowl, and fish quickly or broil them without fat and serve them without heavy sauces. They season with fresh or dried herbs, and flavor with lemon, wine, garlic, and vegetable purees. One interesting aspect of the new cooking is using vegetables for flavoring. Steamed vegetables, whole or pureed, flavored with lemon, herbs, and garlic are served with pasta, rice, or meat.

Most Italians are devotees of raw vegetables dipped in zesty sauces served as antipasto and called *"in pinzimonio,"* which literally means eating with two fingers or pincers. A platter of *"in pinzimonio"* is a palette of colorful, raw or lightly steamed vegetables. Instead of the traditional very salty olive-oil dip, more delicate sauces used in this book are now flavored with fresh sage, bright green basil, rosemary, flat Italian parsley, and a whiff of garlic. *Peperonata*—peppers with onions and tomatoes—is also one of the favorites. *Fagiolini in umido* (string beans with tomato and basil), *finocchio al burro* (braised fennel with a light butter sauce), *spinaci saltiti* (lightly sautéed spinach, a version of spinach à la Florentine) are some of the marvelously fragrant dishes that belong to *cucina magra*.

Dry white wine is also used to enhance taste. Meat is braised in wine; fowl and fish are poached in it. The wine is then thickened with a beaten egg yolk and served as sauce. What an easy way to give substance to a sauce! Huge salads with light Italian dressings, and vegetables raw, steamed, or baked are all part of the "new cooking" concept.

Baked eggs, omelets, eggs with vegetables and cheese are also part of the regime. Low-fat ricotta is used as a thickening agent for sauces and salad dressing.

For those who cannot live without their *dolci,* lean ricotta is made into a fluffy, velvety cream, and water ices are replacing *gelato*—the sinfully rich ice cream. Fruit and cheese have always been favored in Italy as a fitting finale to a repast, and today more than ever they are found on most dining tables.

CUCINA MAGRA PRINCIPLES

Ovid said it, "Stop short of appetite; and eat less than you are able." That's exactly what *cucina magra* or *cucina sana* is all about—cutting down on quantities of food and caloric intake without going on one of the crash or fad diets. Eating smaller portions and sticking to a regime of less fat, less sugar, and pasta without the rich sauces will take weight off gradually, easily, in a healthful enjoyable way without a feeling of deprivation. And you will be able to maintain your weight loss comfortably.

Eating this new Italian way, in addition to introducing you to an exciting cuisine, will renew your appreciation of healthy, fresh, everyday foods. You may even try to follow the Italian daily menu pattern of:

Prima Colazione: A frugal continental breakfast: small glass of juice, coffee and rolls. You may use a bit of butter with the rolls, but no jams or preserves. In spite of the fact that most diets advocate a substantial breakfast, it seems that *prima colazione* works well for exponents of *cucina magra.*

Colazione or Pranzo: A midday lunch may be a light repast of a pasta dish with vegetables, followed by a *granita* (ice) or fruit. Or it may be a cup of *minestra* (soup) without pasta, followed by an egg or vegetable dish, cheese and/or fruit.

Others eat a large midday meal (*pranzo*), that customarily consists of 3 courses, followed by fruit and cheese and sometimes by a sweet.

Pranzo: However, lately, *pranzo* has become the evening meal enjoyed by the entire family; it may consist of 5 or more courses.

On festive occasions, the evening meal begins with an antipasto that may be as frugal or as elaborate as the budget or diet permits. It may consist of salami, cheeses, pickled vegetables, prosciutto, artichoke hearts, accompanied by oil and vinegar.

Most everyday meals begin with a *primo piatto*—either *minestra* (soup with or without pasta) or *pasta sciutto* (pasta cooked in water and served with a sauce).

Secondi Piatti—the second or main course—depends on the region of Italy, tradition, and availability of ingredients. As meat is too expensive, the main course may consist of fish, poultry, or a *fritatta* (omelet). In the southern part, it may be a dish of pasta (*contorni*) smothered by a substantial sauce that sometimes contains meat.

Vegetables are often served along with this course or may follow in the form of a single raw vegetable or a salad. Like pasta, vegetables are often served with a sauce or an olive oil dip. They also may be deep-fried or stuffed with meat, rice, or a vegetable puree. But the devotees of *cucina magra* try to eliminate the heavy sauces and fried foods.

Dolci—fruit and/or cheese—and a pungent cup of espresso round out the meal. Pastries are mostly reserved for special occasions—many families have their own favorite recipes that go back generations and are guarded with great zeal.

Cena: Supper—follows the pattern of the evening *pranzo;* there is really no difference between the two. It's a question of regional expression, depending on where in Italy you are about to dine.

Italian eating habits may sound terribly fattening; however, when you read the recipes in this book you'll see that even the most fattening dishes have lost most of their caloric content. *Cucina magra* is not a reducing diet per se. It's just a discipline of sensible, interesting eating without too much fat or carbohydrates. The portions are smaller, sauces are leaner, cheeses and other dairy products are low-fat, and there is a minimum of desserts. Every food-stuff group is represented and utilized to its best advantage.

When planning your *cucina magra* meals take into consideration your entire family and their nutritional needs, also their likes and dislikes, and the amount of food each of your family members can or should have.

A great variety of foods and different dishes in this book will allow you to please most of your family's and friends' taste and keep the menus varied and exciting.

You can immediately begin to convert your favorite recipes into healthful, nutritional dishes by following a few simple suggestions:

1. Cook soups and stews in advance. Refrigerate and remove the fatty film that has formed on top. Reheat and serve.
2. Instead of sautéeing vegetables, poach them in small amounts of broth with fresh herbs and spices. They will taste so good you don't have to add butter. If you wish, add a light lemon or herb sauce Italian style.
3. Use tuna fish, salmon, or sardines packed in water, not oil.
4. Cut off all fat from meat and poultry before cooking.
5. When you have to sauté, reduce the amount of oil or butter by ⅔, exactly as we have done in most of the recipes. You may also use a pan with nonstick surface which reduces or even eliminates the need for fat.
6. If meat is browned before cooking, drain off all fat before adding vegetables.
7. Use only light olive oil, lemon juice, and herbs for flavoring.

8. When broiling, baking or cooking fish, meat, or fowl on top of the stove, use chicken or beef broth and wine and eliminate or reduce considerably the amounts of butter or oil.
9. Serve *small* portions of pasta with our light freshly made sauces.
10. If you wish to further reduce calories, use cornstarch instead of flour as a thickening agent. You will need only half the original amount when using cornstarch.

If at all possible, grow fresh herbs in your yard, garden or on your window sill; or find out which Italian grocery carries these taste pleasers. Basil, marjoram, oregano, flat-leaf parsley, and mint will add real Italian flavor to your *cucina magra*.

But don't limit yourself to only these herbs. We have provided you with a list of other Italian favorites (page 13).

Have a few basic ingredients for "cooking Italiano" whenever you feel like it. In your cupboard or pantry keep anchovies, artichoke hearts, tuna, ripe olives, a few cans of plum tomatoes, the light Italian or French olive oil, capers, garlic, small amounts of dry Italian herbs and spices, and a good assortment of different pastas for days when you cannot make your own fresh pasta.

In your refrigerator, keep well-wrapped chunks of Parmesan and Romano cheeses that can be grated on a moment's notice. Low-fat ricotta cheese is dated for freshness now, so is mozzarella, and both will keep quite a long time in the refrigerator.

Remember there are no rigid rules attached to Italian cooking. Mamma uses whatever is available and adds a bit of this and a bit of that—plus love, which is the most essential ingredient of "cooking Italiano" and *cucina magra*.

HERBS, SPICES,
AND FLAVORINGS

Aniseed (anice)—with the aroma of licorice, complements cheeses and seafoods.

Basil (basilico)—fresh and dried, one of the most popular Italian spices.

Bay Leaf (alloro)—used either whole or crushed, fresh or dried to enhance flavor of roasts, fish, stews, and soups.

Black Pepper (pepe)—freshly ground with a pepper mill; or used whole.

Chervil (cerfoglio)—fresh or dried, used in many dishes: eggs, meats, fish, and sauces.

Cloves (chiodi de garofoni)—used whole or ground for flavoring tomato juice, chocolate, fruit compotes; some soups, sauces, poultry, and meat dishes.

Coriander (coriandolo)—either whole or crushed, reminiscent of lemon peel or sage. Use in marinades, also for poultry and grilled meats.

Fresh and Dried Mushrooms (funghi)—marvelous for sauces, risottos, pastas, omelettes and soups.

Garlic (aglio)—whole, sliced, crushed, minced, and chopped; used in many recipes, especially in the southern regions.

Lemon (limone)—used to enhance flavor in a multitude of dishes.

Marjoram and Oregano (maggiorana and origano)—related favorites. Marjoram is used more in northern regions; oregano is used extensively in southern dishes.

Mint (menta)—favorite herb of the Roman Empire. Used in fruit drinks and salads, and with poultry and fish.

Nutmeg (noce moscata)—used in egg and spinach dishes, meat sauces, and vegetables.

Parsley (prezzemolo)—sprigs or chopped; flat-leaf Italian parsley should be used in Italian dishes.

Rosemary (rosmarino)—used for beef, lamb, fish and chicken.

Saffron (zafferano)—used in the risottos of the North; pilafs, fish soups, and chicken dishes.

Sage (salvia)—a great favorite for poultry and veal, especially when cooked with wine.

Tarragon (targone)—used for egg dishes, fish, and chicken.

Thyme (timo)—fresh whole leaves, or dried, used for seafoods, fish, cheese dishes, eggs, meats, and soups.

ITALIAN CHEESES
(AN ABBREVIATED LIST)

Asiago: Made from 2 cow milkings. It is a sharp, hard, and granular cheese.

Bel Paese: A soft smooth milk-cheese made in the north of Italy. It is now also made in Wisconsin and Brazil.

Caciocavallo: Resembles a tapering beet root. A delicious smoked cheese, best served for dessert with small crackers.

Fontina: A delectable, semisoft cheese, made in Val d'Aosta. Marvelous with fruit, for sandwiches, but also used in many dishes.

Gorgonzola: Lightly spiced, blue veined cheese, which originated in Milan, but is now produced mainly in the Po Valley. One of the most popular dessert cheeses.

Mozzarella: Made from cow's or water buffalo's milk. It has a slightly sour taste.

Parmigiano Reggiano: It is the original Italian Parmesan. Used mainly for seasoning. It is produced in northern Italy only between April and November. Parmesan should always be freshly grated. Fresh Parmesan, when just cut, is also an excellent eating cheese.

Pecorino Romano: Made from fresh sheep's milk, and curdled with lamb rennet. It is sharp and flavorful. Interchangeable with Parmesan in many dishes; it is used to add flavoring to pasta and sauces.

Provolone: Unaged, it is sweet, delicate, and creamy. Delicious as dessert cheese, also used in cooking. When aged, it becomes sharp and spicy. It is sold in many shapes—fashioned into little pigs, sausages, melons, pears.

Ricotta: A variety of cottage cheese. Made very soft or firm, and used in many Italian dishes, including desserts.

Stracchino: A tangy goat's milk cheese, usually served with peaches, pears, or grapes.

Taleggio: Originated in Bergamo but now is made in many other parts of Italy. Produced from salted curd and has a pleasant aromatic flavor.

ESSENTIAL UTENSILS
FOR ITALIAN COOKING

A good *pastry board*

A 24" long and 2" thick *rolling pin* with tapered ends for pasta

Pasta stamps for cutting and sealing ravioli or *cappelletti*

Ravioli Chef (optional) for easy making of ravioli

Dough and pizza cutter

2" cookie cutters—plain and fancy

Spaghetti pot with colanders; one large colander that fits into the pot snuggly. To drain pasta: lift the colander out of the pot, leaving the water behind.

The small colander has tiny holes so small pastas won't fall through and an overhead handle for easy lifting. The pot lid should have vents for letting out steam. For steaming vegetables, close the vents.

1 large pot without insert

Pasta Tongs and *Spaghetti Rake*

2 pasta forks

Perforated spoons

Cheese grater with its own bowl or container

Spremipomodoro for pureeing fresh tomatoes

Garlic press

Meat mallet for pounding veal cutlets, etc.

Food processor (optional) for easy pasta dough making and pureeing

A blender

A pasta machine that can produce different shaped pastas. It does not have to be expensive or run by electricity, but it's a great helper and also fun to use.

A few sauté pans, large skillets, and stock pots

A good large *colander*

Assorted measuring cups for dry and liquid ingredients

Assorted measuring spoons

3–4 bowls

Wire whisk

Electric hand beater

A good set of *stainless steel knives* for chopping and mincing.

PASTA MEMO

Pasta is a kind of all-encompassing name for the multishaped, farinaceous delicacies from Italy, most often made from semolina, water, and eggs.

Macaroni, spaghetti, noodles, dumplings are all—so much pasta! Pasta is produced in a mind-boggling array of shapes and sizes, all with different names. There is no guarantee that a particular pasta will bear the same name here and abroad. In Italy the names vary from province to province, city to city, and even from store to store. Certainly the best-tasting pasta is the homemade variety. However, today, many stores carry freshly made pasta and many of the prepackaged products are excellent. But stay away from the so-called "instant cooking, starch-free" pastas; your taste buds will be the happier for it.

The secret of really good pasta is in the cooking:

For 1 pound homemade or store-bought pasta, use a large pot, preferably with a perforated insert (page 15) that holds at least 6 quarts water.

Add 1½–2 tablespoons salt, bring to boil and without breaking up the pasta, plunge it into the boiling water, pushing it down as much as possible. Do not stir it with a wooden spoon; separate gently with a pasta fork or the spaghetti rake (page 16).

To always have a perfectly separated spaghetti or any of the other noodles, add 1–2 tablespoons olive or vegetable oil to the water.

Cook store-bought pasta as directed on the package. But to test for doneness, whether your pasta is homemade or store-bought, tasting is the best. (The Italians prefer their noodles al dente—a bit undercooked. However, many people like their noodles a bit softer. Therefore the taste test.)

After boiling pasta for a few minutes, remove a few strands and taste. The thinner or smaller the noodles, the shorter time it takes for them to cook. The thicker ones like ziti or rigatoni will take much longer to be tender.

When done, if you are using a pot with an insert, just lift out the pasta and let the water drain off; or, drain it in a colander. Then place onto a large platter to be tossed with butter, cheese or sauce. Or, remove long strands of spaghetti *or* linguine *from the water with a fork and place right on individual heated plates with melted butter or sauce. If cooking rounded varieties, remove with a slotted spoon. Offer freshly ground cheese and a peppermill on the side.*

We are listing a few of the most popular pastas, grouped into categories: Pasta for Soup, Pasta for Boiling, Pasta for Stuffing, and Pasta for Baking.

Pasta for Soup

Acini de Pepe—"peppercorns"
Anelli—"rings"
Anellini—"little rings"
Capelli d'Angelo—"angel's hair"
Capelli de Pagliaccio—"clown's hats"
Capellini—"fine hairs"; very fine spaghetti-like pasta
Conchigliette—"tiny shells"
Raviolini—small ravioli stuffed with cheese or meat
Spaghettini—spaghetti broken into little pieces
Vermicelli—very thin spaghetti

Pasta for Boiling

Ditali & Ditalini—"thimbles" and "little thimbles"; very short macaroni
Farfalle—"butterflies" or "bows"; these come in several sizes.
Fettuccelle—"little ribbons"
Fettuccine—"small ribbons"; one of the best-known noodles
Fusilli—"twists"; spaghetti made like corkscrews
Gnocchi—dumplings
Lingue di Passeri—"sparrow's tongues"; a wider type of linguine

Linguine—is in the spaghetti family but is a narrow thick noodle.

Macaroni—a name for a large variety of hollow pasta tubes. In this group are ziti, zitoni, tufoli, mezzani, and mezzani tagliati.

Maruzze—"sea shells"

Maruzelle—"small sea shells"

Rigati—"grooved pasta." But this name may be applied to any pasta which has grooves in it.

Rigatoni—also "grooved pasta." Usually large hollow tubes of pasta.

Spaghetti—the name of the famous pasta which actually means "cord or string."

Tagliatelle—these are really no different from *fettuccine,* except that they are wider.

Vermicelli—"little worms"—a very thin spaghetti

Pasta for Baking

Capelletti—"little hats"; curled stuffed pasta which may be boiled or baked.

Elbow Macaroni—curved, hollow pasta tubes.

Farfalle—"butterflies or bows"; may be boiled or baked.

Lasagna—very wide pasta

Lasagne Riccie—wide noodles with one or both sides rippled.

Rigatoni—large grooved noodles suitable for both boiling and baking.

Ziti and Ziti Rigati—"bridegrooms and grooved bridegrooms"; suitable for both boiling and baking.

Pasta for Stuffing

Agnolotti—ravioli with one side rounded; filled with meat or cheese.

Cannelloni—"large reeds"; sold as large hollow tubes, however real *cannelloni,* if homemade, are flat squares of pasta rolled and stuffed.

Manicotti—"small tubes," but also may be made from squares of homemade pasta or sometimes crepes are used and stuffed.

Maruzze (shells) or also sometimes called *Lumache* (snails) that are customarily stuffed.

Ravioli—stuffed squares of pasta that come in many sizes. May be stuffed with cheese, vegetables, or meat.

Tortellini—"small half-moons twisted." Usually stuffed with cheese or meat.

ITALIAN WINE MEMO

In ancient times, Italy was called *"Enotria,"* the land of wine. As the Roman empire grew, vines from Rome were carried to Gaul (France), Iberia (Spain), and Germany. Exportation of Italian wine preceded the culinary exploits of expatriated Florentine chefs (whom Catherine de Medici brought with her to France during the Renaissance) by 1500 years.

Many of the vines that are still cultivated in Italy today were developed during the Middle Ages and the Renaissance, when Tuscany became the most important wine-growing center in the world. However Tuscan wines did not travel well, even with inventions that were supposed to protect the wine—such as a flask with pockets for ice or hot water.

Lacking good wine, other regions of Italy were spurred on to local production; Piedmont, Verona, around Lake Garda, Emilia Romagna, Montefiascone in the Roman Hills and Sicily were among the front-runners.

Now wine is produced all over Italy—each with its own character, bouquet, and flavor. Stretching from the towering Alps to almost within sight of Africa, Italy has a wide range of climate, soil and terrain. As a matter of fact, there is a greater variety of wines produced in Italy than any place in the world.

Italian wines are not only different from wines of other countries, but there is a marked difference between northern, southern, or central Italian wines.

The wines of Italy, like its cuisine, are charming, captivating, and unique. Here is an abbreviated list of wines that you may enjoy with your newly found *cucina magra*.

White Wines

Asprinio—produced near Naples; a dry white wine, excellent with fish; it is known for its peculiar sparkling quality.

Brolio Bianco—produced around Siena; has a remarkable, fresh, crisp taste; excellent with veal, poultry, seafood; also as an aperitif.

Est! Est!! Est!!!—produced near Rome near Lago di Bolsena. Wine with a pronounced flavor of muscat and a very pleasing bouquet. Good with veal, poultry, and fish.

Lagrima d'Arno—produced in Tuscany along the Arno River; a very dry white wine; good with seafood or poultry.

Lagrima Christi—produced near Pompeii; also called *Lacrima Christi;* a light crisp wine with a lovely bouquet; marvelous with fish and shellfish.

Lambrusco—produced in Emilia-Romagna; it has a rich, flowery bouquet and also a light sparkle. Excellent with pasta dishes and poultry.

Orvieto—produced in Umbria, packaged in straw-covered bottles like Chianti, it comes both in Secco (dry) or Abboccato (lightly sweet); the Secco is good with poultry or seafood; Abboccato is sometimes served as a dessert wine, but may also be served with veal, poultry, or pork.

Pinot Grigio—produced near Friuli; amber in color, with a strong bouquet; it has a full-bodied taste; good with fish or seafood.

Prosecco—produced in Venetia; a frothy, light, sparkling wine; it is demi-sec and is bottled in champagne bottles; good with poultry, fish and seafood.

Soave—produced near Lake Garda and Verona, in northern Italy; one of the best-known Italian wines; full-bodied, fresh-tasting wine, best served when very young; good with poultry, fish, seafood, and pasta dishes.

Verdicchio—produced near Ancona; a dry fruity wine made from a rare type of grape, bottled in an amphora-shaped bottle. Good with veal, poultry, game, and seafood.

Red Wines

Amarone—produced near Verona; it is made from the same grapes used for Valpolicella and is one of the classic wines of Italy; good with cheeses and red meats.

Barbaresco—produced in Piedmont, near Turin; has a marvelous bouquet and is a smooth, full-bodied red. Good with steaks, roasts, strong cheeses, and game.

Bardolino—produced around Lake Garda; clear, light-bodied wine with a fruity taste; good with veal, lamb, and pastas.

Barolo—produced in Piedmont; considered one of the

finest wines of Italy; may be consumed young, but it does improve with age; good with red meats, stews, venison.

Chianti—produced in Tuscany; one of the best-known Italian wines; mostly sold young. It has a fruity, fresh taste; when aged, it mellows and acquires body; it is bottled, then, in regular wine bottles and not the familiar, straw-covered bottle of the young wine; good with pasta, red meats, or any Italian food.

Gattinara—produced near Lake Maggiore (northern Italy); the wine is good when young, but when aged about 3 years, it becomes smooth and full-bodied; good with red meats, pastas, game, and cheeses.

Grignolino—produced near Turin (northern Italy); a good quality red with a fresh taste; good with red meats and pastas.

Lambrusco—produced near Bologna; it comes in dry, and slightly sweet, varieties. It has a fine fruity taste and, quite often, a light sparkle; good with red meats, pasta, and cheeses.

Valpolicella—produced near Verona; a lovely, crisp, fragrant wine with a great bouquet; considered one of the finest Italian wines; good with red meats, pasta and cheeses.

Rosé ("When in doubt which wine to serve—serve Rosé")

Antinori Rosé—a light fruity wine with a lovely taste.

Chiaretto del Garda—very light rosé, low in alcohol content, refreshing during hot weather.

Ravello—a sweet tasty rosé; its clean fruity taste makes it a good accompaniment for desserts.

Rosatello Ruffino—a light fruity, light-pink wine, good with all kinds of food.

Dessert and Sparkling Wines

Asti Spumante—a sparkling wine that has been mistakenly compared to champagne. It has a distinctive quality all its own. Made from muscat grapes; it is on the sweet side and a lovely after-dinner wine.

Bracchetto—a bright red wine, quite low in alcohol, with a sweet and velvety taste; a fine after-dinner wine.

Malvasia—produced on the island of Stromboli, near Sicily; it has a pungent, sweet taste and golden-yellow color, made from dry rather than fresh grapes.

Marsala—Sicily's best-known wine produced in sweet, medium, and dry and fortified with alcohol. It is somewhat similar to sherry or Madeira.

(Antipasti)

APPETIZERS

serves 6   **CAPONATA MAGRA I** *Eggplant*

Appetizer

1 large eggplant
1 large onion, minced
3 tomatoes, coarsely
chopped
½ tsp salt
¼ tsp black pepper
2 cloves garlic, crushed
3 Tbs lemon juice
1 Tbs wine vinegar
1 Tbs vegetable oil
1 Tbs minced fresh basil
(or 1 tsp dry basil)
½ tsp oregano

Wash eggplant and pat dry. Bake in 375° oven for about 20 minutes or until soft to the touch.

Cool eggplant, peel, and chop fine. Place in a cheesecloth or sieve and press out excess water. Place in blender with remaining ingredients and blend until mixture is smooth. Adjust seasoning.

Chill and serve as a dip for fresh vegetables or on lettuce as an appetizer.

CAPONATA MAGRA II *Eggplant*
Appetizer

3 large eggplants, peeled
and cut into ½-in cubes
Salt
½ cup olive oil
2 cups finely chopped celery
2 large finely chopped
onions
½ cup wine vinegar
3 cups canned plum Italian
tomatoes, drained and sliced
3 Tbs tomato paste
6 green olives, pitted
and slivered
6 large black olives, pitted
and slivered
2 Tbs capers
4 flat anchovy fillets, well
rinsed and pounded smooth
with a mortar and pestle, or
mashed with a fork in a small
bowl
1¼ tsp salt
½ tsp freshly ground
black pepper
¼ cup pine nuts

Sprinkle the eggplant cubes generously with salt. Place on paper towels for 20 minutes. Pat the cubes dry with fresh paper towels.

In a heavy skillet heat 2 tablespoons olive oil. Add the celery and onions and cook over low heat, stirring frequently, until tender. With a slotted spoon, transfer them to a bowl.

Pour the remaining olive oil into the skillet. Over high heat sauté the eggplant cubes, turning them frequently until they are lightly browned.* Drain on paper towels and squeeze out the oil.

Transfer eggplant back to the skillet and add the celery and onions. Add the vinegar, tomatoes, tomato paste, green olives, black olives, capers, anchovies, salt, and pepper. Bring to boil, reduce heat, simmer uncovered, stirring frequently, for about 20 minutes.

Add pine nuts. Taste the mixture and season with salt and pepper and a little extra vinegar if needed.

Transfer the *caponata* to a serving bowl and refrigerate until ready to serve.

*NOTE: Do not add extra oil if the skillet becomes dry. Squeeze the oil out of the eggplant cubes that are already cooked back into the skillet.

ANTIPASTO DI PEPERONI E FONTINA *Fontina Cheese and Red Pepper Antipasto*

serves 6

4 large red bell peppers
1 head escarole lettuce,
torn into small pieces
10 scallions, chopped fine
2 stalks celery, diced

If you have a gas stove, roast peppers over a flame until blistered on all sides. Hold under cold running water to peel. Discard seeds and membrane. Cut into long strips, ¼" wide.

3 flat anchovy fillets, chopped
5 oz Fontina cheese, thinly sliced

If your stove is electric, preheat oven to 350°. Place peppers on a cookie sheet and bake for 30–35 minutes. Remove from cookie sheet and wrap in a damp towel for ten minutes. Peel skins and slice, as above.

Refrigerate until ready to use.

DRESSING
3 Tbs lemon juice*
3 Tbs vinegar
2 tsp mustard
¼ tsp salt
⅛ tsp pepper
4 Tbs olive oil

In a bowl mix lemon juice, vinegar, mustard, salt, and pepper; add oil, beating steadily until well blended.

In a large salad bowl toss lettuce, scallions, celery, anchovies, and sliced peppers with the dressing. Reserve some peppers for decoration. Place cheese slices and remaining pepper slices on top of the tossed salad.

Serve immediately.

*NOTE: You may wish to use only 2 tablespoons each of lemon juice and vinegar.

PEPERONI ALLA BAGNA CAUDA
Sweet Peppers with Piedmont Garlic and Anchovy Sauce

serves 6–8

8 green peppers
Boiling water
2 Tbs butter
2 Tbs olive oil
4 cloves garlic, minced
8 flat anchovy fillets, minced

Wash the peppers. Drop into a pot of boiling water, reduce heat and simmer for 2–3 minutes. Take off heat and let stand in water for about 10 minutes.

Cut peppers in half. Peel off the skin, remove seeds and fibers, cut into narrow strips and reserve.

In a skillet heat butter and oil together, add garlic and sauté carefully without letting it brown. Take skillet off the heat and add the anchovies. Beat and stir with a wooden spoon. Place on low heat and continue stirring and beating until the mixture is smooth and pastelike.

Place the peppers in a serving dish and pour the hot anchovy mixture over the peppers. Cool and refrigerate.

Serve with Italian bread or bread sticks.

*NOTE: The sauce may also be served hot in a fondue dish, placed over low flame. Sliced raw peppers, celery, mushrooms, cauliflower, or bread cubes may be dipped into the sauce.

FUNGHI RIPIENI *Stuffed Mushrooms*

serves 6–8

24 large mushrooms
1 Tbs vegetable oil
1 small onion, finely chopped
2 Tbs water
2 Tbs Marsala wine
¼ cup fine, dry bread crumbs
¼ cup grated Parmesan cheese

Cut off mushroom stems and reserve. Wipe mushroom caps with a damp cloth and pat dry. Brush caps with vegetable oil. Place hollow-side up in a baking pan and set aside.

Mince mushroom stems and squeeze them dry in a kitchen towel. Simmer onion in the 2 tablespoons water until soft. Add mushroom stems and cook over

¼ cup low-fat ricotta cheese
4 Tbs minced parsley
½ tsp oregano
¼ tsp pepper
1 Tbs margarine, melted

high heat, stirring frequently, for about 5 minutes or until moisture has evaporated.

Add the Marsala and cook until it has nearly evaporated. Remove from heat.

Add bread crumbs, cheeses, parsley, oregano, pepper, and melted margarine. Fill mushroom caps with the mixture.

Preheat oven to 375°. Bake mushroom caps for 15 minutes or until the caps are tender and the stuffing is slightly browned.

Serve immediately.

serves 6

VONGOLE REGANATE *Baked Clams*

36 hard-shell clams
½ cup finely chopped parsley
3 cloves garlic, minced
½ cup grated Parmesan cheese
¼ tsp freshly ground black pepper
½ tsp oregano
½ tsp sweet basil
2 Tbs olive oil
¼ cup bread crumbs

Thoroughly scrub the clams under cold running water. Dry and place in a skillet. Cover. Cook over low heat until shells open.

Discard the top shells. Arrange clams on the remaining half shell in a baking dish.

In a bowl mix parsley, garlic, cheese, pepper, oregano, and basil. Sprinkle this mixture over the clams, then sprinkle with oil and bread crumbs.

Bake in a 425° oven 6–7 minutes. Serve immediately.

serves 6 # ANTIPASTO GIARDINIERA *Garden Antipasto*

4 carrots
1 bunch celery
3 small zucchini
3 red and/or green bell peppers
1 small cauliflower
1 small broccoli
MARINADE
8 cups water
2 cups vinegar
2 Tbs salt
2 Tbs mustard seeds
1 cup sugar
½ tsp rosemary
½ tsp basil
4 large cloves garlic
3 small hot dried red peppers
½ cup stuffed green olives

Scrape carrots and celery and cut into even sticks about 3″ long. Cut unpeeled zucchini into sticks, as well. Cut peppers into strips about ¼″ wide. Break cauliflower and broccoli into flowerettes.

Pour water and vinegar into a large pot. Add salt, mustard seeds, sugar, rosemary, and basil and boil for 3 minutes. Add vegetables and cook for 2 minutes. Drain, reserving marinade. Return marinade to pot and simmer for 15 minutes.

Use 3 or 4 sterilized quart jars. Place a clove of garlic and a dried red pepper into each jar, then pack the vegetables, including olives into jar. Immediately pour marinade into each jar and seal.

The vegetables keep for several months, but allow them to mellow for at least two weeks before serving.

PEPERONI CON TONNO E CAP-PERI *Sweet Peppers with Tuna Fish and Capers*

serves 7–8

3 large red and 3 green bell peppers
3 Tbs olive oil
Juice of 1 lemon
2 cloves garlic, crushed
Salt and pepper to taste
1 7-oz can tuna fish, drained (packed in water)
2 Tbs drained capers
Parsley sprigs to garnish

Broil the peppers under a broiler, turning from time to time, until the skins are scorched and blistered all over, about 10 minutes. When cool enough to handle, peel the skins, then cut each pepper lengthwise into 3 strips and discard stem, pith and seeds.

Put the strips into a bowl. Add oil, lemon juice, garlic, and a little salt and pepper. Let marinate for 30 minutes, stirring occasionally.

Drain, reserving the marinade. Lay the pepper strips flat on a board.

Flake the tuna fish and add the capers. Place a spoonful on each pepper strip and roll up. Arrange the rolls in a shallow serving dish.

Pour the marinade over peppers and serve garnished with parsley.

PEPERONATA *Peppers with Tomatoes and Onions*

serves 6

**9 large peppers; 3 red, 3 yellow, and 3 green
3 Tbs oil
2 large onions, chopped
3 cloves garlic, minced
2 bay leaves
1½ lbs tomatoes, peeled* and sliced
Salt and pepper to taste**

Cut the peppers lengthwise in half; discard the pith and seeds. Cut into ½"-wide strips.

Heat the oil in a skillet and sauté the onions, garlic, and bay leaves for about 5 minutes, stirring occasionally.

Add the peppers, stir, cover and cook on low heat for about 10 minutes. Add the tomatoes, salt and pepper and cook uncovered, stirring frequently, until most of the liquid has evaporated and the *peperonata* is thick.

Remove the bay leaves, taste for seasoning and serve hot or cold.

*NOTE: See peeling instructions (p. 47).

PEPERONATA TUSCANY STYLE

serves 6

**2 mild onions, sliced into thin strips
1 Tbs butter
2 Tbs olive oil
*4 green bell peppers, sliced into thin strips
4 red bell peppers, sliced into thin strips
Salt and pepper to taste
1 tsp fresh basil or ½ tsp dry basil
8 large ripe tomatoes, peeled** and finely chopped
2 cloves garlic**

In a skillet sauté onions in butter and oil until just limp.

Add the peppers, salt, pepper, and basil. Cover and simmer for about 10 minutes; add tomatoes and garlic. Cover and cook for 30 minutes.

Peperonata may be served hot or cold.

*NOTE: All green or all red peppers may be used.

**NOTE: Peeling instructions (p. 47).

MUSHROOMS FILLED
WITH FISH ROE

serves 4–6

24 fresh medium
mushroom caps
½ cup vinegar
¼ tsp oregano
¼ tsp tarragon
¼ tsp black pepper
½ tsp salt

Place mushrooms in a bowl, add all the ingredients and marinate in the refrigerator for 3–4 hours or overnight.

FILLING
¼ lb. fresh fish roe
Water and salt
¼ cup mayonnaise
1 Tbs chopped scallions
1 Tbs chopped dill
1 Tbs lemon juice
Parsley for decoration
Pimiento slices

Poach roe in salted water for 5 minutes. Drain well and cool.

Add remaining ingredients and blend into a very smooth paste. Add salt if necessary.

Drain mushroom caps. Fill each cap with the roe mixture and decorate with parsley and a small piece of pimiento.

Chill for at least 1 hour and serve on lettuce leaves.

ARTICHOKES STUFFED
WITH CRAB MEAT

serves 4

1 can artichokes,
packed in water
1 8-oz pkg frozen crabmeat
⅓ cup Green Dip (page 35)

Drain the artichokes and separate the leaves, forming a hole in the center.

Defrost and shred the crab meat and drain well, add the dip and toss together.

Stuff the artichokes with crabmeat and chill.

CANTALOUPE AND
PROSCIUTTO HAM

makes 24 pieces

1½ ripe cantaloupes
12 thin slices
prosciutto ham

Cut the cantaloupe into slices, 2½" wide and about ¾" thick. Cut the ham slices in half and wrap each piece of cantaloupe with a piece of ham. Spear with a tooth pick.

Chill for ½ hour and serve.

For Hors D'Oeuvres RAW VEGETABLE PLATTER

Asparagus
Small red tomatoes
Scallions
Yellow squash, sliced
Belgian endive, separated
Radishes
Green beans
Carrot curls and
baby carrots
Zucchini, sliced
Broccoli flowerettes
Mushrooms
Cauliflower flowerettes

Arrange all vegetables on a large platter and serve with dips (below) of your choice.

ITALIAN DIP
½ cup light olive oil
3 Tbs wine vinegar
2 Tbs lemon juice
3 cloves garlic, mashed
½ tsp basil
½ tsp oregano
3 Tbs minced scallions
2 Tbs minced parsley
½ tsp salt
¼ tsp black pepper

Place all ingredients into a blender. Blend at high speed for a few seconds. Pour into a bowl and serve with the raw vegetables.

FRENCH DIP
½ cup mayonnaise
1 Tbs lemon juice
2 Tbs tomato paste
1 Tbs wine vinegar or more
1 tsp prepared mustard
¼ tsp finely ground
white pepper
¼ tsp tarragon
2 cloves garlic, crushed

Place all ingredients in blender to blend or mix in a bowl. Refrigerate and serve with the raw vegetables.

GREEN DIP
½ cup yogurt
2 Tbs apple cider vinegar
1 Tbs lemon juice
2 Tbs mayonnaise
2 Tbs chopped scallions
2 Tbs chopped dill
⅓ cup watercress leaves
½ tsp salt
¼ tsp white pepper

Place all ingredients in blender and blend until smooth. Taste for salt and pepper. Refrigerate and serve with the raw vegetables.

makes about 2½ cups
1 pkg low-calorie Italian
dressing mix
½ cup minced cucumber
½ cup minced green pepper
½ cup minced red pepper
1½ cups plain yogurt
2 Tbs lemon juice
½ tsp basil
½ tsp rosemary, crushed

Combine dressing mix with cucumber, green pepper, and red pepper. Fold into the yogurt. Add lemon juice and seasonings. Blend gently with a spoon.

Serve as a dip for raw vegetables or as a salad dressing.

serves 4

STUFFED PEPPERS

1 red pepper
1 green pepper
8 oz low-fat
ricotta cheese
2 Tbs minced pimiento
2 Tbs minced parsley
2 Tbs minced scallions
¼ tsp salt
⅛ tsp white pepper
2 tsp lemon juice
1 envelope unflavored
gelatin
½ cup cold water
Lettuce leaves—use Bibb
or Boston lettuce

Wash peppers. Cut tops off and remove membranes and seeds.

Press ricotta through a sieve into a bowl. Add pimiento, parsley, scallions, salt, pepper, and lemon juice.

Soak gelatin in cold water and melt completely over low heat. Add to cheese mixture.

Fill peppers with cheese mixture and refrigerate for at least 3 hours.

Remove from refrigerator and cut each pepper horizontally into 4 thick slices. Serve 2 slices per person on lettuce leaves.

(Minestre e Minestrone)

SOUPS

ZUPPA DI BROCCOLI *Broccoli Soup*

serves 6

1 Tbs olive oil
2 medium onions, minced
1 garlic clove, minced
½ cup diced prosciutto ham
Black pepper to taste
6 cups water
1 bunch broccoli
1 Tbs butter
4 cups chicken broth
½ cup spaghettini in
1½-in pieces
¼ cup grated
Romano cheese

In a large pot heat oil and sauté onions, garlic, and prosciutto until soft. Add pepper and 4 cups of the water. Simmer, covered, for 20 minutes.

Use just the flowerettes of the broccoli; wash them and cook in 2 cups water until crisp.

Add the drained broccoli to onions, garlic, and prosciutto mixture. Add the chicken broth and spaghettini. Cook for 6–8 minutes.

Serve in soup bowls with Romano cheese.

ZUPPA DI CAPELVENERE E FUNGHI *Fine Noodle and Mushroom Soup*

serves 6

8 cups chicken broth
1 diced carrot
1 celery stalk, diced
2 Tbs chopped scallions
½ tsp salt
10 mushrooms, sliced
¼ lb vermicelli

Bring the broth to boil, add carrots, celery, scallions and salt. Simmer for 12 minutes.

Add mushrooms and vermicelli. Stir well. Cook for about 15 minutes and serve in hot bowls.

SPAGHETTINI IN BRODO *Spaghettini in Broth*

serves 6

1 cup spaghettini in 1½-in pieces
1 qt water, salted
8 cups chicken broth
2 eggs, well beaten
⅓ cup grated Romano cheese

Cook spaghettini *al dente* in salted water and drain.

Bring chicken broth to boil; add spaghettini. Remove from heat and add the beaten eggs, stirring rapidly until the eggs float in strings.

Serve sprinkled with Romano cheese.

MINESTRONE ALLA CASALINGA *Homestyle Minestrone*

serves 8

½ cup navy beans
Water to cover beans
1 Tbs oil
2 onions, chopped
2 cloves garlic, crushed
4 tomatoes, chopped
8 cups water
1 tsp chopped fresh marjoram or 1 tsp dry marjoram
1 tsp chopped fresh thyme or 1 tsp dry thyme
2 carrots, diced
2 potatoes, diced
1 small turnip, diced
2 stalks celery, finely sliced
3 cups grated cabbage
½ cup macaroni pieces or small pasta shells, stars, etc.
1 Tbs chopped fresh parsley
Salt and black pepper to taste
Grated parmesan cheese

Soak the beans overnight in cold water.

Heat the oil in a large pot, add onions and garlic and sauté for a few minutes. Add the tomatoes, beans, water, marjoram, and thyme and simmer covered for about 2 hours.

Add carrots, cook for about 15 minutes, then add the potatoes and turnip. Cook for a few more minutes and add celery, cabbage and pasta.

Cook until the pasta and all the vegetables are tender, about 10–15 minutes. Then add parsley, salt, and pepper to taste.

Serve sprinkled with Parmesan cheese.

serves 6 # ZUPPA DI PESCE *Fish Soup*

2 Tbs olive oil
2 large onions, thinly sliced
2 stalks celery, thinly sliced
3 cloves garlic, finely chopped
3 Tbs chopped fresh parsley
1 cup dry white wine
2 cups chopped tomatoes (fresh or canned)
2 cups fish stock or clam juice
Salt & black pepper to taste
3 lbs fresh fillets (use sea bass, flounder, red snapper)
1 cup small shrimp, cooked and shelled
1 Tbs fresh minced basil or 1 tsp dry basil

Heat the oil in a large pot and sauté onions, celery, and garlic until just tender. Add parsley and wine and bring to boil. Cook 10 minutes.

Add tomatoes, fish stock, salt, and pepper to taste and simmer for 15 minutes.

Cut the fish into thick slices, add to the pot and simmer for 10 minutes. Add shrimp and basil and simmer for another 3–5 minutes.

Taste for seasoning and serve in hot soup bowls.

serves 6 # ZUPPA DI FUNGHI *Mushroom Soup*

1½ Tbs margarine
2 large onions, chopped
1 lb mushrooms, chopped
½ tsp salt
2 cloves garlic, minced
3 cups chicken broth
1 cup water
1 tsp Italian seasoning
3 Tbs yogurt

Heat the margarine in a saucepan. Add onions and sauté until golden.

Add mushrooms, salt, and garlic and cook for 3 minutes, stirring occasionally. Add broth and water and cook for 30 minutes, stirring occasionally.

Before serving place ½ tablespoon yogurt in each soup plate, pour soup over it and mix.

serves 6 # CHILLED SPINACH SOUP

4 cups chicken broth
2 10-oz pkgs frozen
chopped spinach
2 Tbs minced scallions
3 cloves garlic, mashed
1½ cups yogurt
Salt and pepper to taste

Bring broth to boil in saucepan. Add the frozen spinach and bring to boil again, breaking the spinach apart with a fork. Add scallions and garlic and simmer for 4–5 minutes.

Purée mixture in a blender, a little at a time. Add yogurt, a small amount at a time, and blend well. Add salt and pepper to taste.

Refrigerate 3 hours before serving.

serves 6–8 # ZUCCHINI SOUP

1 medium onion, chopped
fine
1 Tbs light olive oil
5 medium zucchini, sliced
¼ tsp thyme
¼ tsp rosemary
¼ tsp basil
¼ tsp salt
⅛ tsp pepper
6 cups chicken broth
1 cup skim milk
2 Tbs minced dill
plus extra for garnish

In a large pot sauté onion in oil. Add zucchini, herbs, and salt and pepper; cook 3–4 minutes, stirring occasionally. Add chicken broth and simmer for 15–20 minutes.

Purée in blender or food processor.

Add milk and dill; then heat but do not boil.

Serve hot or cold sprinkled with additional minced dill.

serves 6 # FRESH TOMATO SOUP

6 medium tomatoes,
coarsely chopped
1 large onion, chopped
2 stalks celery, chopped
2 cups chicken broth
1 Tbs tomato paste
½ tsp basil
½ tsp oregano
¼ tsp sage
¼ tsp freshly ground pepper
½ tsp salt
½ cup whipped cream
or sour cream
2 Tbs chives, minced

Place all the ingredients except cream and chives in a saucepan. Simmer uncovered for 40 minutes, stirring occasionally.

Strain through a fine sieve. Adjust seasoning.

Reheat soup and serve topped with a spoonful of cream and minced chives.

serves 6 # ZUPPA DI COZZE *Mussel Soup*

1 28-oz can Italian plum tomatoes or 3½ cups fresh ripe tomatoes
3 Tbs minced parsley
1 clove garlic, minced
Salt and pepper to taste
3 cups chicken broth
3 lbs mussels, scrubbed
2 tsp minced fresh basil or ½ tsp dry basil
½ cup Chianti (red wine)
2 Tbs minced parsley for garnish

Purée the tomatoes in a food mill or a blender. Pour into a pot.

Add parsley, garlic, salt and pepper to taste, and chicken broth. Stir well, bring to boil and cook for 5 minutes if using canned tomatoes, or 10 minutes if using fresh tomatoes.

Add the chicken broth. Add mussels and basil. Cover pot, bring soup to boil again and cook for 4 minutes.

With a slotted spoon, remove all mussels that have not opened and discard. Add wine and simmer for 2 minutes.

Serve mussels and soup in heated soup bowls sprinkled with parsley.

serves 6 # ZUPPA DI FAGIOLI FRESCHI *Fresh Lima Bean Soup*

2 onions, chopped
1 stalk celery, chopped
1 1-lb can Italian plum tomatoes
1½ lbs fresh lima beans, shelled or 2 10-oz pkgs frozen*
2 qts chicken broth
¼ tsp sweet basil
1 head escarole lettuce, shredded
1 tsp salt
⅛ tsp black pepper
½ cup *anellini* (little rings)
Water and salt
¼ cup grated Romano cheese
¼ cup grated Parmesan cheese

Place onions, celery, and tomatoes in a large pot and simmer for 15 minutes, breaking up the tomatoes with a wooden spoon.

Add lima beans and broth and simmer, covered, for 35 minutes or until lima beans are tender. Add basil, shredded lettuce, salt and pepper.

Cook *anellini* separately in boiling salted water, drain and add to the soup. Simmer for 5 minutes, uncovered.

Serve in heated bowls with cheeses on the side.

*NOTE: If using frozen beans, reduce cooking time by 10 minutes.

serves 6 # MINESTRA AL PROSCIUTTO *Ham Soup*

½ lb fresh lima beans
or 1 10-oz pkg frozen
2 stalks celery, chopped
½ head escarole
lettuce, shredded
½ lb spinach, chopped
Salt and pepper to taste
Water to cover
2 white onions, chopped
1 carrot, diced
¼ lb ham, in a chunk
1 pig's foot
Pepper to taste
¼ tsp marjoram
½ cup *conchigliette*
(tiny shells)
Water and salt
⅓ cup grated
Parmesan cheese

In a large pot combine lima beans, celery, escarole, spinach, salt, and pepper. Add enough water to cover the vegetables. Cover pot; bring to a boil, reduce heat and simmer for 10 minutes.

Add onions, carrot, ham, pig's foot, pepper, and marjoram. Simmer for 60 minutes, covered, until pig's foot is tender.

Remove pig's foot and ham chunk, dice both and return them to soup.

Cook the *conchigliette* separately in boiling salted water for 5 minutes, drain and add to soup. Simmer for 7 minutes, uncovered.

Serve in hot soup bowls sprinkled with Parmesan cheese.

serves 6 # RAVIOLINI IN BRODO *Small Ravioli in Broth*

1 recipe Pasta for Ravioli
(page 130)
½ cup low-fat
ricotta cheese
⅓ cup grated
Parmesan cheese
2 egg yolks
1 Tbs chopped Italian
parsley
Salt and pepper to taste
4 qts chicken broth

Make ravioli dough. Then roll out as directed for ravioli (page 126).

In a bowl mix cheeses, egg yolks, and parsley. Add salt and pepper.

Place teaspoonfuls of the cheese filling 1″ apart on 1 sheet of the dough; cover with the other sheet of dough, pressing it around each mound of filling.

Cut into 1″ squares. Seal the squares securely as directed and be sure to let them dry for 35–40 minutes.

Bring ½ the chicken broth to boil. Add raviolini to the broth and cook for 7 minutes. Remove them with a slotted spoon onto paper towels to drain.

In another pot bring remaining broth to a boil. Pour into soup bowls.

Place 6 raviolini in each bowl and serve immediately.

(Insalate)

SALADS

INSALATA DI POMODORI CON BASILICO *Tomato Salad with Basil*

serves 10

3 qts water
10 ripe tomatoes
2 large red onions
16 oz low-fat mozzarella
cheese
1 large Romaine lettuce
Pesto Dressing

Bring water to boil. Drop in tomatoes and leave in for 30 seconds. Remove with a slotted spoon.* Peel tomatoes and cut into thick slices.

Peel onions and slice. Slice mozzarella ¼" thick.

On a round platter or serving dish, place the Romaine leaves. Alternate overlapping slices of tomato, mozzarella, and onion.

Just before serving, add the Dressing.

DRESSING
¼ cup olive oil
½ cup pine nuts
5 cloves garlic
2 cups fresh basil leaves
or 3 Tbs dry basil
½ cup Parmesan cheese
1 bunch parsley with
stems removed
¼ cup white wine vinegar
Salt and pepper to taste

In a food processor or blender, blend oil, pine nuts, garlic, basil, Parmesan cheese, and parsley until smooth. Add wine vinegar, salt and pepper to taste.

*NOTE: This process is what is referred to as Peeling Instructions (for tomatoes) throughout the book.

INSALATA DI POMODORI *Tomato Salad*

serves 6

6 large ripe tomatoes
2 cloves garlic, crushed
1 Tbs olive oil
Salt and pepper to taste
Garnish: 2 Tbs each,
chopped fresh basil, parsley,
and scallions.

Wash and dry the tomatoes and refrigerate until ready to serve. Cut into ¼" thick slices and place on a shallow dish overlapping slightly.

Mix together garlic, oil, and salt and pepper and pour over the tomatoes. Sprinkle with garnish.

serves 6   # CARCIOFI IN SALSA *Artichoke Hearts in Sauce*

2 Tbs olive oil
3 Tbs lemon juice
2 Tbs grated onion
1 bay leaf, crumbled
Salt and black pepper to taste
*18 small artichoke hearts, frozen or canned, drained
2 Tbs chopped parsley

In a bowl mix together olive oil, lemon juice, grated onion, bay leaf, salt and pepper to taste. Add the artichoke hearts, toss lightly and chill for 1–2 hours, stirring occasionally.

Arrange the artichokes in individual dishes and pour marinade over them. Sprinkle with chopped parsley to garnish.

*NOTE: If using frozen artichoke hearts, cook as directed on the package.

serves 4   # INSALATA DI FINOCCHI E CETRIOLI *Fennel and Cucumber Salad*

1 bulb fennel
1 cucumber
2 Tbs olive oil
2 Tbs lemon juice or vinegar
½ tsp salt
½ tsp pepper
1 clove garlic, finely chopped (optional)

Wash fennel and slice it very thin. Peel cucumber and slice very thin.

Thoroughly mix remaining ingredients in bottom of salad bowl. Add fennel and cucumber, toss well and serve.

serves 8   # INSALATA PRIMAVERA *Spring Salad*

4–5 heads Bibb lettuce or 2 heads Romaine
2 16-oz cans artichokes, well drained
2 green peppers, sliced into thin circles
10 scallions, minced
1 cup minced parsley
2 bunches watercress with leaves removed
24 Italian or cherry tomatoes, halved
½ tsp oregano
½ tsp basil

Separate lettuce leaves and wash well. Shake off excess water. Wrap loosely in paper towels and refrigerate for at least 1 hour. While lettuce is crisping prepare the dressing.

In a cup combine oil and garlic; let stand for at least 2 hours. In a jar with a tight lid or a bottle, combine vinegar, mustard, salt, and Italian seasoning and shake until well blended. Add oil, capers, and pickles and shake well again. Use ½ the dressing for the salad. Keep the rest refrigerated. Shake well before using.

½ tsp black pepper
Salt to taste
1 red onion, sliced
in circles
2 hard-boiled eggs,
quartered
1 can flat anchovy
fillets, drained
½ cup grated
Parmesan cheese

DRESSING
½ cup olive oil
2 cloves garlic, mashed
⅓ cup wine vinegar
1 tsp dry mustard
½ tsp salt
1 tsp Italian seasoning
2 Tbs minced capers
2 Tbs minced dill pickles

Place lettuce in a large bowl. Drain artichokes well and cut into 4 slices each. Add rest of ingredients, except onion, hard boiled eggs, anchovies, and cheese. Sprinkle with ½ cup of the dressing, toss lightly, taste for seasoning; add more dressing, salt and pepper, if necessary.

Garnish with onion, eggs and anchovies. Sprinkle with Parmesan cheese. Serve immediately.

SPINACH SALAD

serves 4–6

1 lb spinach
1 large bunch watercress
12–14 black olives, pitted
12 cherry tomatoes, halved

Remove spinach leaves from stems, wash the leaves well and drain. Remove watercress leaves from stems, wash, drain and combine with the spinach. Wrap in a napkin or kitchen towel and refrigerate for 1 hour.

DRESSING
3 Tbs lemon juice
2 Tbs olive oil
2 cloves garlic, crushed
4 Tbs vinegar
½ tsp salt
1 tsp grated lemon rind
1 tsp sugar
½ tsp mustard

In a bowl combine lemon juice, olive oil, garlic, vinegar, salt, lemon rind, sugar, and mustard. Beat well together with a whisk until smooth. Adjust seasoning.

Place the spinach and watercress in a bowl, toss with the dressing and decorate with olives and tomatoes. Serve immediately.

ZUCCHINI SALAD

5–6 medium zucchini
Salt
2 cups water
½ tsp tarragon
⅛ tsp thyme
1 tsp salt
2 bay leaves
2 cloves garlic
6 peppercorns
2–3 Tbs wine vinegar
2–3 Tbs olive oil
2 Tbs minced fresh
basil or 1 tsp dry basil
2 Tbs minced scallions
1 clove garlic, crushed
Juice of 1 lemon
Salt and pepper to taste
12 cherry and/or Italian
tomatoes, halved

Wash the zucchini and cut into long fingers. Place on a board and sprinkle generously with salt. Let stand for 10 minutes. Blot with paper towels.

In a saucepan bring water to boil, add tarragon, thyme, salt, bay leaves, garlic cloves, and peppercorns. Simmer for 15 minutes, add the zucchini and simmer 5 minutes longer. Strain and remove garlic, peppercorns, and bay leaves.

Place in a serving dish or bowl, add vinegar, olive oil, basil, scallions, garlic, lemon juice, salt and pepper to taste. Add the tomatoes, toss and refrigerate before serving.

INSALATA COMPOSTA *Mixed Vegetable Salad*

A cold vegetable salad composed of several fresh vegetables in season.

YOU MAY USE:
Broccoli and
cauliflower flowerettes
Tiny carrots
Green peas
Green beans
Fennel slices
Asparagus tips
Zucchini fingers

Use any vegetables which you like or which are available.

All vegetables should be lightly steamed or boiled in a small amount of water for a few minutes. The vegetables should be crisp, but not raw.

Cool the vegetables and place in circles or rows on individual serving plates or on a platter. Refrigerate, covered with foil, for 2–3 hours.

Serve generously sprinkled with fresh herbs—basil, sage, parsley, and several lemon wedges. Serve a light olive oil on the side and NO VINEGAR.

ITALIAN GREEN SALAD

serves 6–8

1 head escarole lettuce
1 head Romaine lettuce
2 heads Bibb lettuce
2 cups watercress leaves
2 Tbs minced parsley
3 Tbs minced scallions
2 pkgs frozen artichoke
hearts, cooked and chilled
3 stalks celery, chopped
1 large green pepper, sliced
into thin strips
2 cups green peas, cooked
and chilled
Garnish: 3 large tomatoes,
quartered, and watercress
sprigs

Separate all lettuce leaves; wash, spin dry and refrigerate for 15 minutes, or wrap in a towel and refrigerate for 15–20 minutes.

Place lettuce and remaining ingredients in a large salad bowl, add about ½ cup or a little more dressing*. Toss lightly, garnish with tomatoes and watercress and serve.

*NOTE: Use Insalata Primavera Dressing (page 49).

MUSHROOM AND ARTICHOKE SALAD

serves 6

3 cups thinly sliced
fresh mushrooms
2 pkgs frozen artichoke
hearts, cooked and chilled
2 Tbs minced scallions
2 Tbs minced parsley
3 large ripe
tomatoes, diced
Salt and pepper to taste

Place mushrooms in a salad bowl and sprinkle with 3 tablespoons of the dressing (below).

Cut artichokes in half and add to mushrooms, along with the remaining ingredients. Toss gently.

Add dressing, toss, and refrigerate for 30 minutes before serving.

DRESSING
2 Tbs light olive oil
½ cup lemon juice
¼ tsp pepper
½ tsp basil
¼ tsp oregano
½ tsp salt

Combine all ingredients in a jar with a tight lid and shake well. Add as much dressing as needed to the salad.

INSALATA DI LIGURIA *Ligurian Salad*

3 cloves garlic, minced
2 Tbs light olive oil
6 ripe tomatoes,
thinly sliced
1 purple onion, peeled
and thinly sliced
1 large cucumber, peeled
and thinly sliced
1 red pepper, sliced
into thin strips
1 Tbs minced fresh
basil or 1 tsp dry basil
¼ tsp fennel seed
3 flat anchovies, minced
16 black pitted olives,
sliced
Salt and pepper to taste
1 7-oz can tuna, packed
in water, drained and
flaked
Juice of 1 lemon or
more to taste
1 hard-boiled egg, chopped
3 Tbs minced parsley

In a large salad bowl combine garlic and oil; spread the mixture all over the bowl with the back of a wooden spoon.

Place tomatoes, onion, cucumber, red pepper, basil, fennel seeds, anchovies, and olives into the bowl. Toss salad gently with 2 forks.

Sprinkle with salt and pepper, add tuna and toss again. Refrigerate for 1 hour.

Sprinkle generously with ice-cold lemon juice to taste. Toss gently. Sprinkle with minced egg and parsley and serve immediately.

(Legumi)

VEGETABLES

serves 6 # TIMBALLI DI SPINACI *Spinach and Tomato Timbales*

36–40 large whole
spinach leaves
Hot water, salted
6–8 large ripe tomatoes
Salt and pepper to taste
1 tsp oregano
3 cloves garlic, mashed
3 Tbs fresh minced tarragon
1 Tbs dried tarragon
soaked in hot water
and squeezed dry
½ cup grated
Parmesan cheese

6 5-in baking dishes
with 2–2½-in sides

Remove stems from spinach leaves. Wash leaves under cold running water, without tearing or bruising them. Drop spinach leaves, a few at a time, into boiling salted water for 2 minutes. Remove with a slotted spoon onto paper towels to drain. Set aside to cool.

Chop the tomatoes, cook for 10–15 minutes, add salt, pepper, oregano and garlic and cook until slightly thickened. Pour into a sieve and let drain thoroughly. Add the tarragon and toss lightly.

Line the baking dishes with spinach leaves. Overlap the spinach, covering the bottom and sides of the dishes completely. The leaves should extend beyond the baking dishes.

Fill each spinach-lined baking dish ¾ full with tomato mixture. Reserve 6 tablespoons of tomato for topping.

Fold the spinach leaves over the tomato mixture and top with the reserved tomatoes.

Bake in a preheated 350° oven for 15 minutes. Sprinkle with Parmesan cheese and bake for an additional 5 minutes.

Serve immediately with 2 Italian bread sticks.

*NOTE: You may also serve the timbales cold. Refrigerate for 2–3 hours after baking. Sprinkle with lemon juice and serve as an appetizer or salad.

FUNGHI IN UMIDO ALLA VERONESE *Verona-Style Mushrooms*

serves 6

2½ cups mushroom caps
1 Tbs olive oil
1 Tbs butter
1 large onion, finely
chopped
2 cloves garlic, crushed
2 Tbs chopped fresh parsley
½ tsp thyme
½ tsp marjoram
1 Tbs flour
2 Tbs lemon juice
Salt and black pepper
to taste

Wash and pat dry the mushroom caps and slice.

Heat oil and butter in a saucepan and sauté onion, garlic, and parsley for about 6 minutes.

Add thyme and marjoram. Sprinkle with flour and cook for 1 minute. Then add mushrooms and simmer for about 1–2 minutes, until they are tender.

Add lemon juice, salt and pepper to taste. Bring to boil and remove from heat.

Serve over pasta or with meat or fish.

ZUCCHINI RIPIENI *Stuffed Zucchini*

serves 6

6 zucchini, about
5–6 in long
Salted water
1 slice white bread
with crust removed
¼ cup milk for soaking
¼ lb low-fat ricotta
¼ tsp oregano
1 clove garlic, crushed
⅓ cup grated
Parmesan cheese
1 egg yolk
Salt and pepper to taste
1 Tbs oil

Wash and trim zucchini. Drop them into a pot of boiling salted water, simmer for 5 minutes and drain.

Soak bread in milk, then squeeze dry.

Cut zucchini in half lengthwise and scoop out the centers, using a teaspoon. Chop the centers and put them into a bowl.

Add bread, ricotta, oregano, garlic, Parmesan cheese, egg yolk, salt and pepper to taste. Mix thoroughly. The mixture should be soft; if it seems too stiff, add a little milk.

Fill zucchini cases and level stuffing. Place close together in a single layer in an oiled, shallow baking dish.

Cook in a preheated 375° oven for 35–40 minutes until zucchini are tender and the filling is golden brown.

v. good

serves 6 # MELANZANE ALLA PARMIGIANA
*Eggplant
Parmesan*

2 eggplants, peeled
Salt
2–3 Tbs olive oil
6 oz low-fat mozzarella
cheese
2 cups Tomato Sauce (page
109)
½ cup freshly grated
Parmesan cheese

Slice eggplants into circles, ¼″ thick. Place on paper towels and generously sprinkle with salt. Cover and leave to stand for 25 minutes. Press each slice between paper towels to drain.

works well

Oil a large baking pan with some of the olive oil. Place eggplant in a single layer in the pan and brush lightly with oil. Bake in a preheated 400° oven for about 10 minutes or until browned. Turn and bake until browned on the other side.

Cut the mozzarella into thin slices.

Spread a thin layer of tomato sauce in the bottom of an ovenproof serving dish and place a layer of eggplant slices over the tomato sauce. Pour more tomato sauce over the eggplant. Top with ½ the mozzarella slices. Repeat the layers.

Bake in a preheated 400° oven for 20 minutes. Sprinkle with the Parmesan cheese and bake for 10–15 minutes longer until the cheese is golden brown.

serves 6 # ZUCCHINI ALLA FIUME *Zucchini Fiume Style*

6 medium zucchini
3 cups water
1 Tbs cider vinegar
½ tsp salt
1 tsp paprika
1 tsp flour
1 cup yogurt
2 Tbs chopped dill

Pare zucchini and cut into long narrow strips like spaghetti.

Bring water to boil, drop in zucchini and boil for 5 minutes. Drain.

Place in a saucepan, sprinkle with the vinegar, salt, and paprika and simmer for 7 minutes. Toss lightly, being careful not to break the zucchini. Dust with the flour, toss again, then add the yogurt.

Heat to boiling point but do not boil. Add dill, mix and serve.

PISELLI AL PROSCIUTTO *Braised Peas with Prosciutto*

2 Tbs butter
1 medium onion, finely chopped
¼ cup chicken broth
2½ cups shelled young peas or 2 12-oz pkgs frozen peas, thawed
¼ cup lean prosciutto, cut into thin strips
Salt and pepper to taste

Melt the butter in a saucepan and sauté the onion gently for 5–6 minutes until transparent.

Add the broth and peas, bring to boil, cover and simmer for 15 minutes. (For frozen peas follow timing on the package, allowing even less time if the peas are thawed.)

Add prosciutto and cook, uncovered, stirring frequently, until the liquid is absorbed. Add salt and pepper to taste.

serves 6 # POMODORI COL RISO *Tomatoes Stuffed with Rice*

6 large firm tomatoes
½ cup raw rice
2 cloves garlic, crushed
1 Tbs olive oil
1 Tbs chopped fresh basil or 1 tsp dry basil
2 Tbs water
Salt and pepper to taste
Garnish: small parsley sprigs

Cut a slice off the top of each tomato and reserve. Using a teaspoon, scoop out the pulp and discard the hard central core.

Place pulp in a bowl. Add the rice, garlic, oil, basil, water and salt and pepper. Mix well.

Sprinkle inside of tomatoes with salt and place them in a baking dish. Fill each tomato ⅔ with the tomato-rice mixture. Replace the "lids" so that the rice is completely covered. Cover the dish with foil and bake in a 350° oven for about 1 hour.

Garnish each tomato with a sprig of parsley and serve immediately.

serves 6 # SPINACI SALTITI *Sautéed Spinach*

3 qts water
2 Tbs salt
2½ lbs fresh spinach
2 Tbs olive oil
2 cloves garlic, mashed
⅛ tsp nutmeg
Salt and pepper to taste
½ cup toasted pine nuts
(optional)

In a large pot bring water to boil, add salt.

Remove stems from spinach and wash well. Drop into boiling water. Cook for 15 minutes. Drain and cool. Chop coarsely and squeeze dry.

Heat olive oil in a skillet, add mashed garlic and cook for 1 minute. Add spinach, nutmeg, salt and pepper, toss. Cook over medium heat for 4–5 minutes.

Serve immediately. If desired, sprinkle with pine nuts.

serves 4 # GREEN BEANS WITH CHERVIL

1 pkg (9 oz) frozen
whole green beans
1 tsp fresh chervil,
minced, or ½ tsp
dry chervil
2 tsp butter
or margarine

Cook green beans as directed on the package. Drain and toss with chervil. Add butter and toss again.

EGGPLANT AND ZUCCHINI BAKE

serves 6

3 medium zucchini
1 medium eggplant
2 Tbs salt
3 ripe tomatoes,
peeled* and thinly sliced
12 mushrooms,
thinly sliced
1 large onion,
thinly sliced
Salt and pepper to taste
2 Tbs light olive oil
3 Tbs lemon juice
1 clove garlic, minced
½ tsp basil
½ tsp oregano

Peel zucchini and eggplant and cut into slices, ¼" thick. Place on paper towels and sprinkle generously with salt. Cover and let stand for 15 minutes. Blot dry with paper towels.

Place a layer of zucchini and eggplant into a shallow baking dish. Then a layer of tomatoes, mushrooms, and onions. Sprinkle each layer with salt and pepper.

In a measuring cup or a small bowl, mix together oil, lemon juice, garlic, basil and oregano. Pour over the onions.

Cover pan with foil and bake in a preheated 450° oven for 15 minutes. Reduce heat to 350° and bake for another 20 minutes. Uncover and bake for 20 minutes.

Serve hot.

*NOTE: Peeling instructions (p. 47).

PUREE OF CARROTS

serves 6

2 lbs carrots,
scraped and sliced thin
Water and 2 tsp salt
Salt and pepper to taste
1 Tbs melted butter
(optional)
2 Tbs minced parsley

Cook carrots in salted water for 25 minutes or until very tender.

Cool slightly, then puree in a blender or press through a fine sieve. Reheat in the saucepan, stirring continuously. If you wish, add melted butter at the last minute.

Serve sprinkled with parsley.

TURNIPS FLORENTINE

6 medium turnips
1½ qts water and
1 tsp salt
1 Tbs minced onion
1 10-oz pkg frozen
chopped spinach, defrosted
Salt and pepper to taste
1 Tbs butter
or margarine

Peel and wash turnips. Cut each into 4 pieces. Cook, covered, in salted water with onion for 30 minutes or until very tender.

Drain and cool turnips and press through a sieve.

Place mashed turnips and defrosted spinach into a saucepan, add salt and pepper, stir well and cook over low heat for 5–6 minutes.

Add butter, stir well and serve hot.

PUREE OF GREEN BEANS

2 lbs fresh green beans,
snapped, or 3 10-oz
pkgs frozen
Water and 1½ tsp salt
Salt and pepper to taste
2–3 Tbs lemon juice
1 Tbs crumbled bacon
or bacon bits

Wash and cut beans into ½–1″ pieces. Cook in salted water uncovered for 10–15 minutes or until tender. (Cook frozen beans as directed on the package.)

Drain, but reserve ½ cup of cooking liquid. Rinse beans in cold water. Puree in a blender with lemon juice and the cooking liquid, small amounts at a time, until very smooth. Add salt and pepper to taste.

Reheat in a saucepan and serve sprinkled with bacon.

(Uova e Frittate)

EGG DISHES

serves 6 # FRITTATA DI ZUCCHINI *Zucchini Omelet*

2 Tbs olive oil
5 scallions, finely chopped
2 cloves garlic, mashed
4 tender small zucchini, thinly sliced
2 large tomatoes, chopped
1 Tbs minced parsley
½ tsp thyme
½ tsp marjoram
Salt and pepper to taste

In a large skillet heat oil, add scallions and garlic and cook until tender, about 6 minutes. Add remaining ingredients. Stir, cover and cook until zucchini is tender, and most of the liquid has evaporated, about 6–8 minutes.

Cool completely.

OMELET
8 eggs
2 Tbs water
Salt and pepper to taste
2 Tbs butter
Grated Parmesan cheese (optional)

Beat the eggs and water slightly. Add the vegetables and salt and pepper and mix gently.

Melt the butter in a 9″ skillet with an ovenproof handle. Pour egg mixture into the skillet. Cook until the edges of the omelet pull away from the skillet and the underside is brown.

Place under the broiler for 1–2 minutes to brown the top.

Cut into wedges and serve immediately. If you wish, serve grated Parmesan cheese on the side.

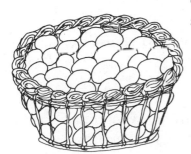

FRITTATA DI PORRI *Hearty Omelet with Leeks*

6 large leeks,
white part only
6 cups cold water
2 tsp salt
3 Tbs light olive oil
8 eggs
Salt and black pepper to taste
1 tsp minced fresh sage
or ¼ tsp dry sage

Preheat oven to 350°.

Wash leeks thoroughly. Cut off the green part and reserve for soups or sauces. Cut the white part into ½" circles.

Place leek circles into a bowl with the water and 2 teaspoons salt. Soak for 10 minutes. Drain in a colander and then on a triple thickness of paper towels.

In a skillet heat 1 tablespoon of the oil, add leeks and cook over medium heat, stirring occasionally, for about 20–25 minutes or until tender. Set aside to cool.

In a large bowl beat eggs with salt, pepper, and sage. Add cooled leeks and blend well.

In a 10" skillet with an ovenproof handle, heat remaining 2 tablespoons oil and pour in egg mixture. Cook over low heat for 30 seconds. With a fork lift the sides of the omelet, tilt pan, and let eggs flow under the set part. Cook over medium heat for 3 minutes.

Place skillet into preheated oven and bake for 7–8 minutes or until the eggs are completely set. Loosen all around the pan with a spatula and slide onto a heated platter.

Cut in wedges and serve immediately; or let cool and serve at room temperature.

serves 6 # FRITTATA DI SPINACI *Baked Spinach Omelet*

2 Tbs light olive oil
1 medium onion, thinly sliced
8 eggs
½ lb raw spinach, finely chopped

Preheat oven to 350°.

Heat oil in a 10" skillet with an ovenproof handle. Sauté onion in skillet until pale golden brown.

¼ cup grated
Parmesan cheese
1 Tbs minced parsley
1 clove garlic, minced
Salt and pepper to taste

In a large bowl beat eggs with a whisk until just broken up. Add remaining ingredients and beat with the whisk until well blended.

Pour egg mixture into skillet with the onions. Cook on top of stove for 30 seconds, then lift sides of omelet as it sets; tilt pan and let the uncooked eggs flow under set portion of omelet. Cook for additional 2 minutes over medium heat.

Bake in the preheated oven for 10 minutes. Remove from oven and loosen omelet from pan with a spatula.

Slice into wedges and serve immediately.

serves 8

FRITTATA AL BASILICO *Omelet with Basil*

*½ cup fresh basil leaves
8 eggs
Salt and pepper to taste
3 Tbs Parmesan cheese
2 tsp olive oil

Coarsely chop basil leaves. In a bowl beat the eggs with salt and pepper, add the Parmesan cheese and beat well. Add the basil leaves and stir gently.

In an omelet pan heat the oil and pour in the eggs. Cook until omelet is set and browned on the underside.

Place a plate over the omelet pan. Reverse omelet pan so that omelet falls onto the plate.

Return pan to the stove. Slide omelet into the pan to cook the top side.

In 1–2 minutes slide omelet onto a platter, cut in wedges, and serve hot or cold.

*NOTE: If fresh basil is not available use ⅓ cup fresh parsley and 1 teaspoon dry basil soaked in 1 tablespoon hot water and then squeezed dry.

SCRAMBLED EGGS AND RICOTTA CHEESE

serves 8

3 eggs
6 Tbs water
1 tsp salt
10 oz low-fat ricotta cheese
2 Tbs chopped scallions
1 Tbs margarine

Break eggs into a bowl. Add water and ½ teaspoon salt. Beat lightly with a fork.

Mix ricotta with remaining salt and scallions and set aside.

Heat margarine in a skillet, pour in eggs and cook, stirring constantly with a fork, until just beginning to set.

Pour mixture into a shallow baking dish. Spread cheese over the eggs. Bake in 400° oven for 10 minutes.

EGGS FLORENTINE

serves 6

4 Tbs skim or low-fat milk
2 10-oz pkgs frozen chopped spinach, defrosted
½ tsp salt
½ tsp garlic powder
6 eggs
½ cup low-fat, grated mozzarella cheese

Pour milk into a large skillet and add the spinach. Cover and cook for 10 minutes, stirring occasionally. Sprinkle with salt and garlic powder.

With a large spoon make 6 indentations in the spinach. Break the eggs into the indentations. Cover and cook for 5 minutes.

Sprinkle eggs with grated cheese. Cover again and cook for about 5 minutes or until the cheese has melted.

Serve hot.

FRITTATA SPUMOSA *Frothy Omelet*

serves 3–4

4 egg yolks
1 Tbs heavy cream
½ tsp salt
⅓ cup grated mozzarella or Gruyère cheese
4 egg whites
2 Tbs butter

Beat the egg yolks, cream, and salt until smooth. Stir in cheese.

Beat the egg whites until stiff, but not dry, and fold into egg-yolk mixture.

Melt butter in a 9″ skillet and pour in the eggs. Cook

over low heat for 30 seconds. Lift edges with a fork and tilt pan to allow uncooked eggs to run under.

When the omelet is quite set, fold over and roll out onto a heated platter. Serve immediately.

UOVA IN TAZZINE
serves 6 # CON SPINACI *Eggs and Spinach in Cups*

1½ lbs fresh spinach
or 2 10-oz pkgs
frozen spinach*
4 cups water and 1 tsp salt
Salt and white pepper
to taste
⅛ tsp nutmeg
6 Tbs milk
3 Tbs melted butter
6 slices prosciutto
or cooked ham
6 eggs
6 custard cups

Remove stems from spinach leaves. Wash spinach thoroughly and cook in the salted water for 10 minutes. Drain well and puree in a blender or force through a sieve. Add salt, pepper, nutmeg, and ½ the milk.

Pour ½ tablespoon butter into each custard cup. Divide ½ the spinach between the cups; cover with a slice of ham and top with remaining spinach. Make a slight indentation in the spinach.

Break an egg into a clean cup and discard ½ the egg white. Place egg on top of spinach. Repeat process for each cup.

Sprinkle with salt and pepper, then pour ½ tablespoon of the remaining milk over each egg.

Bake in a 400° oven 6 minutes or until eggs are set.

*NOTE: If using frozen spinach, follow directions on the package.

*(Pesce e
Frutti di Mare)*

FISH
AND SEAFOOD

PESCE AL FORNO CON LIMONE
serves 6

Baked Fish with Lemon and Dill

6 whitefish fillets
(about 1½ lbs)
½ cup white wine
Juice of 1 lemon
2 Tbs chopped fresh dill
1 clove garlic, minced
¼ tsp salt
Garnish: lemon slices and
dill sprigs

Fold fish fillets into thirds and place in a baking pan.

Combine wine, lemon juice, dill and garlic and pour over fish. Bake in a 350° oven for 20–25 minutes or until fish flakes.

Place fish fillets on a serving platter and sprinkle with salt. Garnish with lemon slices and dill sprigs.

SALMONE IN GELATINA *Salmon in Aspic*
serves 6

3 cloves
1 onion, cut in half
2 bay leaves
5 peppercorns
2 stalks celery, sliced
4 sprigs parsley
1 tsp marjoram
Salt to taste
6 cups water
6 fresh salmon steaks,
½" thick
2 Tbs gelatin
½ Tbs lemon juice
Garnish: thin lemon slices

Stick the cloves into onion halves. In a large pot combine onion, bay leaves, peppercorns, celery, parsley, marjoram, and salt. Add the water. Bring to boil and cook over medium heat for 10–15 minutes.

Place salmon in the pot and cook over low heat for 45 minutes. Let cool in the broth for 15 minutes. Carefully remove salmon. Place in a serving dish.

Strain the broth into a bowl. Soften the gelatin in lemon juice. Add to the hot broth and stir until dissolved. Pour a little broth over the fish, and let it set.

Chill remaining gelatin broth until it begins to set, then beat with an electric beater. Place the beaten gelatin in mounds on top of the fish.

Chill and decorate with lemon slices.

serves 6 # PESCE AL FORNO *Baked Fish in Tomato Sauce*

6 slices (2 lbs) fish (haddock, scrod, or whitefish)
2 tsp salt
½ tsp ground pepper
1½ Tbs olive oil
1 medium white onion, chopped
2 stalks celery, chopped
1 green pepper, chopped
2 cups canned whole tomatoes, chopped
2 cloves garlic, minced
1 tsp basil
2 bay leaves, crumbled

Sprinkle fish with salt and ¼ teaspoon ground pepper. Brush baking dish with 1 teaspoon oil; place the fish into baking dish and refrigerate while making sauce.

Heat remaining oil in a saucepan and sauté onion, celery, and green pepper until tender, stirring frequently. Add remaining ground pepper, tomatoes, garlic, basil, and bay leaves. Cook over low heat for 20 minutes, stirring occasionally.

Puree the mixture in a blender or press it through a sieve and then pour over the fish.

Bake in a 350 oven for 45 minutes or until fish flakes easily.

serves 4 # TRIGLIE ALLA CALABRESE *Red Snapper Calabrian Style*

3 lbs red snapper or 2 yellowtails, each about 1½ lbs
Salt and pepper to taste
1 Tbs olive oil
1 Tbs chopped fresh marjoram or 1 tsp dry marjoram
1 Tbs butter
½ cup white wine
2 Tbs capers, drained
8 black olives, chopped
1 Tbs chopped fresh parsley

Buy cleaned whole fish with head and tail on (or clean it yourself). Wash the fish, pat dry and sprinkle the insides with salt and pepper.

Heat oil with marjoram in a large skillet and sauté the fish for 6–8 minutes on each side, turning once.

Cook butter and wine in a small saucepan for 3 minutes. Remove from heat and add capers, olives, and parsley.

Carefully place cooked fish on hot serving platter and pour the hot sauce over fish.

serves 6 ## TROTINE AL FUNGHI *Trout with Mushrooms*

6 trout, about 10 oz each
Salt and pepper to taste
½ cup flour
1 Tbs oil
2 Tbs butter
2 Tbs white wine
2 scallions, finely chopped
3 cups sliced mushrooms
2 Tbs chopped fresh parsley
Juice of ½ lemon
Garnish: lemon quarters and parsley sprigs

Wash trout, leaving the heads and tails on, and pat dry. Season inside and out with salt and pepper; then coat lightly with flour.

Heat oil and butter in a large skillet and sauté the trout for 6–8 minutes on each side, until lightly browned.

In another skillet heat wine and cook scallions and mushrooms until the mushrooms begin to soften, about 3–5 minutes. Add parsley and lemon juice and toss lightly.

Place the trout side by side on a large hot platter with rows of mushrooms between them. Garnish with lemon and parsley.

good w/ rainbow trout fillets (red) served w/ rice + asparagus (e.g.)

serves 6–8 ## BURRIDA *Genoese Fish Stew*

4 lbs various fish fillets
1 Tbs olive oil
2 cloves garlic, chopped
1 large mild onion, chopped fine
2 anchovy fillets, minced
½ cup chopped parsley
*16-oz can sliced, peeled tomatoes
2 cups dry white wine
2 bay leaves
¼ tsp crushed fennel seed
¼ tsp crushed saffron
Salt and pepper to taste
Slices of toasted Italian bread

Use any fish fillets of your choice: whitefish, red snapper, haddock, slices of mackerel, or rock salmon. Cut the fillets into 2½"–3" pieces.

Heat the oil in a heavy pot. Add garlic—do not let it brown. Add onions and cook until just tender. Add anchovies, parsley, tomatoes and their liquid, and wine. Cook for 10 minutes.

Add the fish, bay leaves, fennel seed, saffron and salt and pepper to taste. Simmer for an additional 20 minutes.

Serve in soup bowls with bread slices.

*NOTE: Peeling instructions, page 47.

serves 6 — PESCE AFFOGATO *Poached Fish*

1 stalk celery
1 carrot, scraped
1 small onion, peeled
and stuck with 3 cloves
1 clove garlic
2 bay leaves
4 sprigs parsley
1 cup dry white wine
5 peppercorns
½ tsp rosemary
½ tsp basil
¼ tsp sage
2 tsp salt
8 cups water
6 firm fish fillets
or steaks (haddock, halibut,
or scrod)
Lemon juice for final touch

If you have a fish poacher use it. Or use a large skillet.

Place all ingredients except fish into the poacher or skillet. Cook mixture for 35 minutes on low heat.

Strain through a fine strainer into a container. Return strained liquid to poacher or skillet, add the fish and poach for about 20 minutes over low heat or until fish flakes easily. Add a little salt to taste.

Remove poacher from heat and let fish remain in poacher for 5–6 minutes before serving. Sprinkle with lemon juice and serve with Peperonata (p. 33) or fresh steamed vegetables.

serves 6 — GENOESE SEA BASS

1 Tbs butter
or margarine
6 slices
sea bass, ½″ thick
1 medium onion,
finely chopped
Salt and pepper to taste
½ tsp basil
3 tomatoes, chopped
2 cloves garlic, minced
8 black olives, sliced

Melt the butter in a large skillet; sauté the fish and onion for 6 minutes, turning the fish once.

Add the salt, pepper, basil, tomatoes and garlic. Cover and cook over low heat 15 minutes or until fish flakes easily.

Add olives, cook 2 minutes and serve.

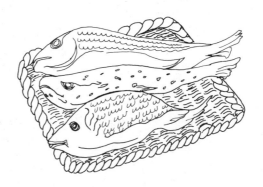

PESCE ITALIANO *Fish Italiano*

2 Tbs light olive oil
2 onions, chopped
3 cloves garlic, minced
½ lb mushrooms, sliced
½ cup capers, drained
1 Tbs flour
6 slices (1½ lbs)
fish fillets (sole,
flounder, or scrod)
¾ cup chicken broth
¼ tsp oregano
1 tsp salt
¼ tsp pepper
3 Tbs minced parsley

Heat olive oil in a large skillet with an ovenproof handle and sauté the onions and garlic until just transparent. Add mushrooms, capers, and sprinkle with flour. Cook over low heat for 5 minutes.

Place the fish on top of the vegetables. Add the broth, oregano, salt, pepper, and parsley. Bake in a 375° oven for 30–35 minutes or until fish flakes easily.

RED SNAPPER GENOA STYLE

2½ lbs red snapper steak
2 green peppers, diced
2 medium onions, diced
2 large tomatoes, diced
¼ tsp oregano
¼ tsp basil
¼ tsp rosemary
Salt and black pepper to
taste
½ cup fish stock or
clam broth
½ cup dry white wine
Lemon slices

Wipe the red snapper steak with damp cloth; sprinkle with salt and pepper to taste. Place fish onto heavy-duty foil.

Arrange peppers, onions, and tomatoes around and over the fish. Sprinkle the vegetables with oregano, basil, rosemary, salt, and pepper. Fold the foil over the fish but do not seal. Pour the fish stock and wine over the fish and vegetables. Now seal the foil.

Wrap an additional piece of foil over the fish if necessary. Place in a baking pan and bake 30 minutes in 400° oven.

Open foil, test red snapper for readiness. Fish is ready when it flakes easily when tested with a fork. Place lemon slices over the fish and cook open for about 5 minutes.

Place on a serving dish, fold back sides of the foil, and serve right out of the foil.

FILETTI DI SOGLIOLA CON
FRUTTI DI MARE *Fillets of Sole with Seafood*

serves 8

3 lbs fillet
of sole
24 medium raw shrimp
½ cup lemon juice
½ tsp salt
¼ tsp white pepper
1 tsp Italian seasonings
4 Tbs butter
1 large onion, chopped
½ lb mushrooms, sliced
1 tsp salt
½ tsp pepper
1 cup tomato purée
⅓ cup dry vermouth
16 frozen artichoke
hearts, thawed
¾ cup low-fat milk
1 small jar pimientos,
chopped
½ cup parsley, chopped

Cut sole fillets into strips about 1" × 2". Shell and devein the shrimp.

Mix lemon juice, salt and white pepper, and seasonings and marinate fish and shrimp for 1 hour, stirring occasionally. Drain well.

In a large skillet heat 2 tablespoons of the butter; add onion, mushrooms, salt and pepper and sauté 5 minutes. Add tomato puree, vermouth, sole and shrimp, and simmer for 5 minutes.

Remove fish with a slotted spoon onto a heated platter.

Heat remaining butter in a saucepan, add artichoke hearts and cook 5 minutes. Add tomato mixture, bring to boil and reduce by about ⅓. Add milk and pimientos and simmer 2 minutes.

To serve; place shrimp on top of sole. Cover with artichoke mixture and garnish with chopped parsley.

serves 6

SALMONE PAESANO *Salmon Peasant*
Style

2 lbs salmon steaks
½ tsp salt
¼ tsp white pepper
1 cup sliced mushrooms
½ cup sliced green onions
¼ cup tomato purée
2 Tbs oil
Garnish: lemon slices

Cut salmon into serving-size portions. Place into a lightly greased 8" × 12" baking dish. Sprinkle with salt and pepper.

Combine remaining ingredients and spread over top of fish.

Bake in a 350° oven for 25–30 minutes or until fish flakes easily when tested with a fork. Garnish with lemon slices.

SHRIMP AND BEANS LIVORNESE

serves 6

1½ tsp chicken broth powder
1 cup boiling water
¼ cup thinly sliced scallions
2 cloves garlic, crushed
1½ lbs raw medium shrimp, peeled and deveined
1 Tbs oil
1 tsp salt
½ tsp basil
½ tsp oregano
1 10-oz pkg frozen cut green beans
2 Tbs minced parsley

Dissolve chicken broth powder in boiling water.

Cook scallions, garlic, and shrimp in oil for 3 minutes, stirring frequently. If necessary, add a little of the chicken broth to prevent sticking.

Add salt, basil, oregano, green beans, and chicken broth. Cover and simmer 5–7 minutes or until beans are cooked but still slightly crisp.

Sprinkle with parsley and serve.

RICE AND SEAFOOD

serves 6

1 Tbs olive oil
1 large onion, diced
2 cloves garlic
3 Tbs water
Salt and pepper to taste
1 large tomato, minced
1 cup rice
½ cup dry white wine
2½ cups water
12 large shrimp, shelled and deveined
12 mussels or clams, debearded and well washed
12 small crayfish well cleaned or ¼ lb sliced, cooked lobster meat*
¼ tsp each rosemary, basil, and thyme
3 Tbs minced parsley

Heat oil in a large, deep skillet. Add the onion, garlic and water. Cover and cook over low heat stirring occasionally for about 3–4 minutes.

Add salt, pepper and tomato, stir and cook 2–3 minutes longer. Add the rice and cook, stirring frequently, for 4–5 minutes.

Add the wine, water, shrimp, mussels and crayfish. Cover and cook until the water has been almost absorbed about 20–25 minutes.

Add seasonings, stir lightly, cover and finish cooking until the rice is fluffy and the crayfish red, about another 5–10 minutes. Sprinkle with parsley and serve.

*NOTE: If using cooked lobster meat, do not add until the last few minutes—along with the seasonings.

serves 6

COZZE AL VERMOUTH *Mussels in Vermouth*

48 mussels
1 cup dry white vermouth
8 shallots or 1
small onion, chopped
1 Tbs butter
2 tsp cornstarch
Salt and pepper to taste
½ tsp fennel seed
2 Tbs chopped parsley

Wash and scrub the mussels and place in a skillet. Add vermouth and shallots.

Cover and cook over high heat for 4–6 minutes or until the mussels open. Remove the mussels with a slotted spoon and keep warm.

Mix butter and cornstarch together and add to the vermouth in the pan. Cook until the sauce thickens slightly. Add salt and pepper, fennel, and parsley. Bring to boil once.

Serve the mussels with some of the sauce in soup plates.

serves 6

RICE AND STEAMED SHRIMP

24 raw large shrimp
in shells
½ bag shrimp spices
3 cups water
3 cups fluffy cooked rice

Wash shrimp.

Place shrimp spices loose (out of bag) into a large skillet, add water and bring to boil. Add shrimp, cover and boil 3–4 minutes or until the shrimp are bright pink.

Remove shrimp with a slotted spoon together with the spices and serve with the rice.

serves 6

SHRIMP SCAMPI

4 Tbs light
olive oil
3 cloves garlic,
finely chopped
3 Tbs minced parsley
18 jumbo shrimp,
shelled and deveined
1 cup pale dry sherry
1 cup chicken broth
or consommé
Salt and pepper to taste
½ tsp basil

Heat olive oil in a large skillet and sauté garlic and 2 tablespoons parsley for 2 minutes. Add shrimp and sauté until pink on both sides.

Add sherry and simmer for about 5 minutes. Add broth. Add salt and pepper and cook 10–15 minutes.

Sprinkle with basil and remaining parsley and serve.

serves 6

SCAMPI ALLA SALSA DI VINO

Shrimp in Wine Sauce

2 Tbs flour
1 tsp salt
½ tsp pepper
1½ lbs uncooked medium
shrimp, shelled
and deveined
2 Tbs light olive oil
1 cup dry white wine
1 Tbs tomato paste
2 scallions, minced
2 Tbs chopped parsley

In a bowl combine flour, salt, and pepper. Add shrimp and toss to coat shrimp.

Heat olive oil in a skillet. Brown shrimp on both sides

In a bowl mix together wine, tomato paste, and scallions; add to the shrimp. Cook over low heat for 6–7 minutes, stirring occasionally.

Sprinkle with the parsley, taste for seasoning and serve.

POULTRY

POLLO ALLA MAMMA CANTONETTI *Chicken Mamma Cantonetti*

serves 4–5

1 chicken, cut up
country style*
Salt
¼ cup lemon juice
½ cup pale dry sherry
½–1 tsp garlic powder
2 tsp Italian seasoning
2 Tbs chopped scallions
2 Tbs chopped parsley

Rub chicken with salt and lemon juice.

Pour sherry into a baking dish, add garlic powder and Italian seasoning. Place chicken in the dish and turn a few times, coating chicken with wine and spices.

Place skin side down, and bake in 375° oven until golden brown, about 45 minutes. Turn skin side up and bake for 10–15 minutes longer to brown the skin, or place under the broiler for a few minutes.

Sprinkle with scallions and parsley and continue baking for another 5 minutes.

*NOTE: cut into 8 pieces with backbones separated.

serves 6 # POLLO ALLA FIORENTINA *Chicken Florentine*

3 chicken breasts,
cut in half
1 Tbs olive oil
1 Tbs butter
2 cups Marinara Sauce
(page 114)
½ cup dry red wine
1½ cups chicken broth,
boiling
1 cup uncooked rice
½ cup sliced black olives
1 10-oz pkg frozen chopped
spinach, thawed and
squeezed dry
1 cup low fat
ricotta cheese
1 egg, well beaten
½ tsp oregano
½ tsp basil
½ tsp salt
¼ tsp nutmeg
¼ cup grated
Parmesan cheese

Preheat oven to 350°.

Heat oil and butter in a saucepan. Brush chicken breasts with the mixture. Place on a grill in a baking pan and broil for about 5 minutes on each side.

In a bowl mix Marinara sauce and wine. Pour 1 cup of this sauce-and-wine mixture into a skillet.

Add chicken broth, rice and olives; stir well, scraping bottom of skillet. Bring to boil and pour into a 3-quart casserole.

Place chicken skin side down on top of rice. Cover tightly with foil and bake 25 minutes. Turn chicken, and bake another 25 minutes.

In the meanwhile, mix spinach, ricotta, egg, and seasonings. Then, pour spinach mixture and remaining sauce-wine mixture over chicken. Sprinkle with Parmesan.

Bake, uncovered, 10–15 minutes.

serves 4–5 # POLLO PICCANTE *Chicken in Spicy Sauce*

1 Tbs olive oil
3½-lb fryer, cut into
serving pieces
4 cloves garlic, minced
1 tsp salt
⅛ tsp pepper
½ tsp sweet basil
½ cup dry white wine
3 Tbs wine vinegar
¼ cup boiling water
3 anchovy fillets, chopped

Heat the oil in a skillet; add chicken and garlic, sprinkle with salt and pepper and brown on all sides over low heat.

Add basil, wine and vinegar; cook 5 minutes. Add the boiling water and chopped anchovies.

Cook over low heat 45 minutes or until chicken is tender. Adjust seasoning.

INVOLTINI DI PETTI DI POLLO

serves 4

Stuffed Chicken Breasts

4 chicken breasts, boned
and skinned
Salt and pepper to taste
4 thin slices boiled ham
4 thin slices Bel
Paese cheese
4 asparagus spears, cooked
½ cup flour
for dusting
1 Tbs butter
1 Tbs oil
4 Tbs Marsala
4 Tbs chicken broth
Garnish: cooked asparagus
spears (fresh or frozen)

Place the chicken breasts between pieces of waxed paper and pound thin with a mallet.

Season with salt and pepper and place a slice of ham on each breast, then a slice of cheese, and an asparagus spear. Roll each breast up carefully and secure with a toothpick. Dust with flour.

Heat butter and oil in a skillet and sauté the chicken rolls on low heat, turning frequently, until tender and browned, about 15 minutes. Transfer the rolls to a hot serving dish and keep warm.

Add the Marsala and broth to the juices in the pan. Bring to boil and simmer 3–4 minutes.

Pour sauce over the rolls and garnish with asparagus spears.

CHICKEN CACCIATORE

serves 4

3 Tbs light olive oil
1 3-lb chicken, cut
into serving pieces
2 cloves garlic
½ tsp salt
¼ tsp pepper
1 tsp rosemary
½ tsp sage
6 anchovy fillets, chopped
⅓ cup wine vinegar
1 cup red wine
3 Tbs tomato paste
½ cup chicken broth

Heat oil in a large skillet and sauté chicken and garlic for 5 minutes. Turn chicken often.

Remove garlic. Add salt, pepper, rosemary, sage, anchovies, wine vinegar, and red wine. Cook, uncovered, until the liquid has been reduced by ⅓.

Dissolve tomato paste in chicken broth and pour over the chicken. Simmer, covered, for 30 minutes or until the chicken is very tender.

serves 4

CHICKEN ITALIANO

2 Tbs light olive oil
1 3-lb chicken, cut
into serving pieces
½ tsp salt
⅛ tsp pepper
1 large green pepper,
sliced into thin strips
1 large onion, sliced
into thin strips
2 cloves garlic, minced
1 16-oz can tomatoes
½ tsp oregano
½ tsp thyme
1 cup sliced mushrooms
2 Tbs minced parsley

Heat oil in a large skillet and brown chicken on all sides for about 15 minutes.

Add all the ingredients except mushrooms and parsley. Cover skillet and simmer for 30 minutes.

Add mushrooms and simmer for 30 minutes or until the mushrooms and chicken are tender. Sprinkle with parsley and serve.

serves 6

CHICKEN IN WHITE WINE AND BRANDY

3 chicken breasts,
split and skinned
2 Tbs light olive oil
¼ lb ham, thinly sliced
4 carrots, scraped and
cut into chunks
18 small white onions,
peeled
2 cloves garlic
¼ tsp thyme
1 bay leaf
3 sprigs parsley
¼ tsp tarragon
1 Tbs tomato paste
½ cup chicken broth
1½ cups white wine
½ tsp salt
¼ tsp pepper
1 Tbs flour
1 Tbs margarine
2 Tbs brandy

In a large pot brown chicken breasts in hot oil. Drain excess fat.

Cut ham into ¼″ strips. Add ham and vegetables to the chicken. Add remaining ingredients except flour, margarine, and brandy. Simmer chicken for 1 hour.

Remove parsley sprigs and bay leaf. Mix flour and margarine until blended. Add to chicken and stir lightly until sauce is thickened.

Add brandy. Simmer 1 minute and serve.

TOMATO CHICKEN

serves 4–5

1 chicken, cut into
serving pieces
1 tsp salt
¼ tsp black pepper
1 Tbs olive oil
1 cup chopped onions
⅓ cup dry white wine
3 Tbs tomato purée
2 tomatoes, sliced
1 clove minced garlic
2 Tbs chopped parsley
½ tsp thyme
½ lb mushrooms, sliced

Sprinkle chicken with salt and pepper. Heat oil in a skillet and brown chicken on all sides.

Add onion, cover and simmer until the onion is tender, about 5–8 minutes. Add the wine, tomato puree, and simmer covered for 15 minutes, turning the chicken occasionally.

Add the sliced tomatoes, garlic, parsley and thyme. Cover and cook for 25 minutes on low heat.

Add the mushrooms, stir well, and simmer another 10–15 minutes.

ANITRA ARROSTO AL MARSALA
Roast Duck with Marsala

serves 3–4

4–5 lb duck
Salt and pepper to taste
1 small onion
1½ tsp sage
3 Tbs Marsala
⅔ cup water
Juice of ¼ lemon

Remove the giblets and wash and dry the duck. Sprinkle the inside with salt and pepper. Place the onion and ½ the sage into the cavity. Prick the skin of the duck to release the fat while cooking, then rub with remaining sage.

Place the duck, breast down, in a roasting pan with the giblets around it. Roast in a preheated 350° oven for 30 minutes.

Turn breast upwards and pour Marsala over the duck. Continue roasting, basting with pan juices now and then, for 1½ hours or until the skin is crisp and golden brown. Transfer the duck to a serving dish and keep warm.

Skim off fat from the roasting pan, add water and lemon juice, bring to boil and taste for seasoning. Strain the sauce into a hot dish and serve with the duck.

serves 6

FILETTI DI TACCHINO AL VINO
Turkey Breasts with Wine

2 lbs boneless turkey
breast, skin removed
Salt and pepper to taste
3 Tbs melted butter
⅔ cup white wine
½ cup chicken broth
1½ cups thinly sliced
mushrooms
Salt and pepper to taste
3 Tbs grated
Parmesan cheese
Garnish: 3 cups cooked
broccoli flowerettes and
lemon wedges

Cut the turkey breast into 6 slices, each ½″ thick. Place the slices between waxed paper and flatten a little with a mallet. Sprinkle with salt and pepper.

In a baking dish combine butter, wine, and chicken broth. Place turkey pieces into the baking dish. Cover with foil and bake in a 375° oven for 45 minutes.

Fold back foil and spread mushrooms over the turkey. Sprinkle mushrooms with salt and pepper, and Parmesan cheese.

Cover again with foil and bake for 20 minutes. Uncover pan and place under a preheated broiler for 1–2 minutes until the cheese is slightly browned.

Serve immediately garnished with broccoli and lemon wedges.

serves 4–5

POLLO ALLA PIEMONTESE *Chicken*
Piedmont Style

4 Tbs lemon juice
½ cup minced onion
3 Tbs minced parsley
1½ tsp salt
3 lb frying chicken, cut
into serving pieces
½ cup sifted flour
½ cup water
1 Tbs olive oil
1 egg white

Mix together lemon juice, onion, parsley and ½ the salt. Rub chicken with the mixture and let stand for 2 hours.

Beat together flour, water, remaining salt, and oil. Let stand 1 hour. Beat the egg white until stiff and fold into flour mixture.

Dip chicken pieces into the mixture coating them well. Place into a lightly greased baking pan. Bake in a 400° oven, turning pieces once.

serves 6–7 # CAPPONE ARROSTO *Roast Capon*

1 5-lb capon
2 tsp salt
Black pepper to taste
3 Tbs brandy
2½ cups chicken broth
2 Tbs butter
1 Tbs flour
1 cup low-fat milk
2 Tbs minced capers
⅛ tsp nutmeg
¼ tsp Italian seasoning
2 Tbs minced parsley

Wash and dry the capon; sprinkle with salt and pepper. Place in a shallow baking pan; roast in a 375° oven for 35 minutes.

In a small pot or ladle, heat brandy until lukewarm, ignite, and pour brandy over capon; when flames die down, add broth to the pan. Reduce heat to 350° and roast 1½ hours longer, or until capon is tender*, basting frequently with pan juices.

Pour out the pan juices and reserve. Skim off the fat.

Melt butter in a saucepan. Add flour, stir and cook for 1 minute. Add the pan juices, stirring constantly, and cook over low heat for 5 minutes. Add milk and cook, stirring steadily until thickened. Add capers, seasonings and parsley.

Serve the capon, sliced, with the sauce over it.

*NOTE: If you wish, insert a meat thermometer into the thickest part of capon breast without touching the bone. Bake until thermometer reaches 175°–poultry.

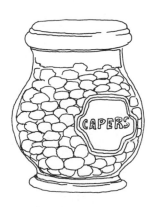

(Carne)

MEATS

BISTECCA ALLA PIZZAIOLA *Beefsteak with Fresh Tomato Sauce*

4 sirloin steaks,
½" thick
Salt and pepper to taste
1 Tbs olive oil
Garnish: parsley sprigs

SAUCE
1 Tbs olive oil
3 cloves garlic, sliced
2½ cups seeded and
chopped tomatoes (fresh
or canned)
1 Tbs fresh basil or
1 tsp dry basil

Sprinkle steaks with salt, pepper, and oil. Let stand for 1 hour at room temperature.

Prepare sauce: heat oil and garlic in a skillet for 1–2 minutes, then add tomatoes, salt and pepper to taste. Bring to boil and cook 5–6 minutes, until the tomatoes are just softened. Add basil and set aside.

Broil steaks 3 minutes on each side. Then place them in a lightly oiled baking pan. Top each steak with a thick layer of the sauce and cover the pan tightly with foil.

Bake in a 350° oven for 15–20 minutes or until the steaks are tender. Garnish with parsley.

serves 6 # MANZO BRASATO AL VINO ROSSO *Beef Braised in Red Wine*

3 lbs top round
roast or brisket
2 onions
1 carrot, sliced
1 stalk celery, sliced
2 bay leaves
6 peppercorns, cracked
2 cups red wine
1 Tbs oil
Salt and pepper to taste

Put the meat into a bowl. Slice 1 of the onions and add along with the carrot, celery, bay leaves, peppercorns and wine to the meat. Cover and marinate in the refrigerator for 24 hours, turning several times.

Remove meat from the marinade and pat dry with paper towels. Reserve the marinade.

Heat oil in a heavy pot. Finely chop the other onion and sauté for about 5 minutes. Add the meat, increase heat and brown the meat on all sides.

Add the strained marinade and bring to boil. Add salt and pepper, lower the heat, cover tightly and simmer for at least 3 hours or until the meat is tender, turning the meat once.

Transfer meat to a serving platter. There should be just enough sauce around the meat to moisten each slice. If there is too much liquid, reduce the sauce by boiling rapidly. If there is not enough liquid, add a little water or wine.

Slice the meat into fairly thick slices. Pour sauce over meat and serve.

STUFFED BEEF ROULADES

serves 6

2 lbs round steak
⅔ cup low-fat mozzarella cheese, grated
1 small onion, chopped
1 stalk celery, chopped
½ tsp thyme
½ tsp sage
¼ cup chopped parsley
2 Tbs olive oil
1 cup beef broth
½ tsp dry mustard
Salt and pepper to taste

Cut meat into 6 pieces and pound each piece to a ¼″ thickness.

In a small bowl combine cheese, onion, celery, thyme, sage, and parsley. Divide mixture into 2 parts. Set aside 1 part.

Place a small amount of cheese mixture in the center of each piece of meat; roll and secure with a tooth-pick.

Heat oil in a large pot and brown meat. Drain excess fat. Mix beef broth and mustard and add to the pot. Cover and simmer for 50 minutes.

Add reserved cheese mixture to the pot and simmer 35 minutes or until meat is tender.

Remove meat to a heated platter. Skim excess fat from pan juices. Over high heat cook pan juices to reduce and thicken. Season to taste and pour over meat rolls.

BEEF WITH VEGETABLES

serves 6

1 red pepper
1 green pepper
1 large onion
3 tomatoes
3 medium zucchini
3 Tbs light olive oil
6 slices round steak,
about 4 oz each
1/2 tsp salt
1/8 tsp pepper
1/4 tsp dry basil
1/4 tsp oregano
2/3 cup white wine

Slice peppers into thin strips. Slice onion into thin strips. Cut tomatoes into eighths. Wash zucchini and cut into 1/4″ slices.

Heat oil in a large skillet and add all the vegetables. Cook for about 10 minutes, stirring occasionally.

Lightly grease an ovenproof baking dish and place 1/2 the vegetable mixture in the bottom. Place steak on top and cover with remaining vegetables. Sprinkle with salt, pepper, basil, and oregano. Add wine. Cover and bake in a preheated 350° oven for 60 minutes.

Ten minutes before completion, remove cover and finish baking uncovered so that excess liquid can evaporate.

STUFFED EGGPLANT

serves 6

1 large eggplant
1 Tbs salt
1 large onion, chopped
1 cup chopped mushrooms
1 lb lean ground beef
2 Tbs light olive oil
2 Tbs tomato paste
1/4 cup bread crumbs
1 tsp basil
1/2 tsp chervil
1/2 tsp salt
1/4 tsp pepper
2 Tbs grated
Parmesan cheese
Garnish: parsley

Wash eggplant and cut in half lengthwise. Remove the pulp, leaving 1/2″ of shell. Sprinkle pulp and inside of shells with 1 tablespoon of salt and set aside for 15 minutes. Blot pulp and shells with paper towels.

In a skillet sauté the onion, mushrooms, and meat in hot oil. Add the tomato paste, crumbs, seasonings, and the eggplant pulp. Cook until no red is visible in the meat.

Place the meat mixture into the eggplant shells. Place filled shells into a greased ovenproof dish. Bake in a preheated 350° oven for 30 minutes.

Sprinkle with cheese and bake 10 minutes longer. Garnish with parsley. Serve hot.

BEEF CARRARA

3 Tbs light olive oil
2 lbs beef stew meat,
cut into cubes
½ cup beef broth
1 cup dry red wine
½ tsp salt
¼ tsp thyme
3 cloves garlic, minced
1 lb small white onions,
peeled and left whole
1 qt water and
1 tsp salt
1 lb small mushrooms
1 tsp sugar
½ cup ripe olives, pitted
1 10-oz pkg frozen
peas, thawed

In a large pot heat 1 tablespoon of the oil and brown the meat.

Add broth, wine, salt, thyme, and garlic. Cover and simmer for 1 hour or until meat is tender. Then cook, uncovered, for 10 minutes to reduce liquid.

Cook the onions in boiling salted water for about 15 minutes or until just tender. Drain.

Slice mushrooms and saute them in remaining 2 tablespoons oil. Remove with slotted spoon; add to the meat.

In the same pan, saute onions until lightly browned. Sprinkle with sugar and heat to glaze. Add to the meat.

Add olives and peas, and simmer for 5 minutes. Serve immediately.

serves 6 # STUFFED GREEN PEPPERS

12 small, light-green
peppers (Italian type)
1 lb lean beef,
ground
¼ cup cooked white rice
1 Tbs bread crumbs
1 egg
½ tsp salt
¼ tsp pepper
1 clove garlic, mashed
2 Tbs cold water

Core peppers, being careful not to tear skin, and set aside.

Prepare stuffing: blend together ground beef, cooked rice, crumbs, egg, salt, pepper, garlic, and cold water.

Stuff the peppers with the mixture, place in a saucepan and pour the Tomato Sauce (below) over the peppers. Simmer for 45 minutes or until peppers are very tender.

TOMATO SAUCE
1 15-oz can plain
tomato sauce
1 clove garlic, crushed
¼ tsp oregano
¼ tsp black pepper
¼ tsp thyme
¼ tsp tarragon

Mix all the ingredients together.

COSTATINE DI MAIALE AL FINOCCHIO *Pork Chops with Fennel*

serves 6

2 Tbs olive oil
6 loin pork chops,
about ½-in thick
Salt and pepper to taste
¼ cup tomato paste
3 Tbs water
⅓ cup dry red wine
2 cloves garlic, minced
½ tsp fennel seeds

Heat oil in a large skillet and brown chops on both sides over medium heat until tender, about 20–25 minutes in all. Sprinkle with salt and pepper. Remove chops from the skillet onto a heated platter and keep warm.

Mix tomato paste with water. Add tomato paste, wine, garlic, and fennel seeds to the skillet. Boil briskly until the sauce has been reduced by about ¼.

Pour sauce over the chops and serve.

MAIALE ALLO SPIEDO *Pork on a Skewer*

serves 6

1 lb pork tenderloin
2 slices bread, ½-in
thick, with crust removed
¼ lb thinly sliced
prosciutto
16 bay leaves
2 Tbs olive oil
Salt and black pepper

Cut pork into 12 cubes. Cut bread into 12 cubes of approximately the same size as the meat. Cut prosciutto into 12 pieces. Divide the pork, bread, prosciutto, and bay leaves equally between 6 metal skewers, stringing them in succession.

Lay the skewers flat, slightly apart, in a baking dish, oiled with 1 tablespoon of the oil. Sprinkle lightly with salt and generously with pepper and sprinkle with remaining oil.

Bake in a preheated 375° oven for 30–40 minutes until the meat is cooked and the bread crisp and crunchy. Turn the skewers once, halfway through cooking. Serve immediately.

MAIALE AL LATTE *Pork Cooked in Milk*

serves 6

2 lbs boneless
loin of pork
Salt and pepper to taste
2 cloves garlic, crushed
½ tsp coriander
1 Tbs butter
4 cups low-fat milk

Season the meat with salt and pepper and rub with garlic and coriander.

Melt butter in a deep, heavy pot. Brown the meat over low heat, turning to brown on all sides.

In a saucepan bring the milk to boil. When the meat has browned, pour the milk over it. Simmer covered for about 1 hour. Stir the milk well and continue cooking 30–45 minutes, until the meat is tender and the milk reduced to about 1 cup.

Lift out the meat, slice and arrange on a hot serving platter, and keep hot.

Stir the milk that remains in the pan and scrape the bottom of the pan. The sauce should be creamy. If it is not, cook for a few more minutes, taking care that it does not burn.

Pour sauce over the slices of pork and serve immediately.

CIMA ALLA GENOVESE RIPIENE
Stuffed Breast of Veal

serves 10–12

2 lb boned breast of veal
pounded to ½-in thickness
Salt and black pepper
to taste
2 slices bread
with crust removed
½ cup milk
2 chicken livers
½ cup water and ¼ tsp salt
1 Tbs butter
1 medium onion,
finely chopped
½ lb ground veal
⅓ cup grated
Parmesan cheese
¼ tsp dry marjoram
½ cup green peas
¼ cup shelled
pistachio nuts

Lay the veal flat on a board. Sprinkle with salt and pepper; fold in half and sew the 2 longer sides together with a strong thread to form a pocket.

Soak bread in the milk until soft, then squeeze dry. Simmer livers in salted water for 3 minutes. Drain and mince. Heat butter in skillet and sauté the onion until just soft. Remove from heat and add the bread, livers, veal, cheese, marjoram, peas, pistachio nuts, beaten egg, and salt and pepper. Mix together lightly but thoroughly.

Stuff ½ the stuffing into the veal pocket; cover with the hard-boiled eggs and remaining stuffing. Carefully sew up the opening to enclose stuffing.

1 egg, lightly beaten
2 hard-boiled eggs, sliced
4–5 veal bones
6–7 cups salted water

Place veal bones in a deep pot. Lay the veal roll on top and cover with cold salted water. Bring to boil, cover and simmer for 1½–2 hours. Leave to cool in water. Drain and refrigerate.

Serve cold, cut into fairly thick slices.

serves 6

ROLLATINI DI VITELLO *Veal Rolls*

1½ lbs veal, sliced
into 12 thin slices
Salt to taste
⅛ tsp finely ground
white pepper
12 very thin slices
baked or boiled ham
12 very thin slices
Swiss cheese
2 Tbs melted butter
2 bay leaves, crumbled
1¼ cups dry vermouth
18 small white onions,
peeled and left whole
2 large tomatoes, cut
into 8 slices each
1 Tbs cornstarch
2 Tbs minced parsley
Garnish: parsley or
watercress

Place each piece of veal between two sheets of waxed paper. With a mallet pound gently to a ¼″ thickness. Remove wax paper and sprinkle veal with salt and pepper.

Place a slice of ham, then a slice of cheese on each piece of veal. Roll up veal with ham and cheese on the in-side. Secure with wooden toothpicks.

Pour melted butter into a shallow baking pan. Add bay leaves and 1 cup vermouth. Place veal rolls into the pan. Cover with foil and bake for 15 minutes in a 375° oven.

Add onions to veal rolls. Bake covered for about 30 minutes or until onions are just tender. Add tomatoes to the pan during the last 10 minutes of baking.

With a slotted spoon, remove veal rolls and place on a serving platter; remove picks. Place vegetables around veal rolls. Keep warm.

In a small bowl combine cornstarch and remaining vermouth; mix until smooth. Add vermouth mixture to pan juices. Pour into a saucepan. Cook, stirring often, for 3 minutes. Pour sauce over veal rolls.

Sprinkle veal with minced parsley; garnish with watercress.

VEAL PICCATA

2 Tbs butter
2½ lbs sliced veal,
pounded thin
1 cup dry white wine
Salt and pepper to taste
1 lemon, thinly sliced
2 Tbs minced parsley

Melt butter in a skillet. When it bubbles, sauté veal on both sides until golden brown. Add wine, and salt and pepper to taste. Cook for 5 minutes.

Remove veal and place on a serving platter. Place a thin slice of lemon on each piece of veal and sprinkle with parsley.

Cook pan juices until reduced by about ⅓. Pour over the veal slices.

COSTOLETTE DI VITELLO
VALDOSTANA *Stuffed Veal Chops*

serves 8

8 loin veal chops,
cut ¾-in thick
8 slices prosciutto ham
8 slices low-fat
mozzarella cheese
½ tsp salt
½ tsp black pepper
3 Tbs butter
½ cup dry white wine
¼ tsp rosemary

Cut a pocket in each chop horizontally through the middle. Pound the chops lightly.

Place a slice of prosciutto and cheese into each pocket, squeeze the edges closed and secure with toothpicks. Sprinkle with salt and pepper.

Heat butter in a large skillet and sauté the veal until browned on both sides. Add wine and rosemary; cover and cook over low heat 30 minutes or until tender.

VEAL CUTLETS WITH CAPERS

serves 6

very tasty

turkey/chicken 6 veal cutlets,
about 5 oz each
3 Tbs lemon juice
yes ½ tsp salt
⅛ tsp pepper
½ tsp paprika
2 Tbs light olive oil
several T. ½ cup capers, drained
⅓ cup dry vermouth
1 bay leaf
4 Tbs evaporated
(skim) milk

Make more sauce than this!

Sprinkle cutlets with lemon juice, salt, pepper, and paprika, *generously*

Heat oil in a skillet and sauté cutlets for 3 minutes on 1 side. Turn cutlets and add the capers. Cook again for 3 minutes. Remove cutlets with a slotted spoon and place on a heated platter.

Pour vermouth into the skillet, scraping loose any brown particles from the bottom. Add bay leaf and

If turkey cut fairly thick, stays moist & tender

simmer for 4 minutes. Remove bay leaf; add evaporated milk and cook for 2–3 minutes.

Pour sauce over cutlets and serve immediately.

ARTICHOKES AND VEAL

serves 6

2 cloves garlic, chopped
1 Tbs light olive oil
1½ lbs veal round, cut into small pieces and pounded thin
½ tsp salt
⅛ tsp pepper
1 16-oz can tomatoes, drained and chopped
⅓ cup dry white wine
¼ tsp oregano
¼ tsp basil
1 10-oz pkg frozen artichoke hearts, defrosted

In a large skillet sauté the garlic in oil until light brown. With a slotted spoon remove garlic and discard.

Sprinkle veal with salt and pepper. Sauté in the oil. Add tomatoes, wine, oregano, basil, and mix well.

Add the artichoke hearts, cover and simmer for 1 hour or until the meat is tender.

VEAL SCALLOPINI WITH TOMATOES

serves 6

1½ lbs veal, thinly sliced and pounded thin
2 Tbs light olive oil
½ lb mushrooms, thinly sliced
2 cloves garlic, mashed
2 Tbs minced parsley
1 Tbs minced fresh basil or 1 tsp dry basil
1 large tomato, diced
½ cup dry white wine
2 Tbs Parmesan cheese

In an ovenproof pot sauté veal on top of the stove in hot oil until golden brown on both sides.

Add the remaining ingredients, except Parmesan cheese, and stir well. Cover and bake in a 350° oven for 30 minutes.

Sprinkle with Parmesan cheese and bake, uncovered, 10 minutes longer.

VEAL STUFFINO

serves 6

1½ lbs veal shoulder,
cut into cubes
2 Tbs light olive oil
1 carrot, minced
2 stalks celery, minced
1 onion, minced
2 cloves garlic, minced
½ cup dry vermouth
2 tomatoes, finely chopped
½ tsp salt
¼ tsp pepper

In a large skillet sauté veal in hot oil.

Add carrot, celery, onion, garlic, and vermouth. Stir well. Simmer for 5 minutes. Add tomatoes, salt, and pepper. Cover and simmer on low heat for 1½ hours.

Add more liquid from time to time if the veal seems dry. If there is too much liquid, uncover and cook over high heat for a few minutes to reduce the liquid.

Serve immediately.

AGNELLO CON PEPERONI *Lamb with Sweet Peppers*

serves 6

6 loin lamb chops
Salt and pepper
1 Tbs olive oil
2 cloves garlic, crushed
1¼ cups dry white wine
6 peppers (mixed green
and red if available),
cut into chunks
4 tomatoes, quartered
1 bay leaf
½ tsp oregano

Trim excess fat from chops and sprinkle with salt and pepper. Heat olive oil with garlic in a large skillet, add the meat and sauté until lightly browned, turning once or twice.

Add wine and cook on high heat for 5 minutes. Add the peppers, tomatoes, bay leaf and oregano. Cover tightly and simmer for 45 minutes or until lamb is tender.

Check the seasoning and serve from the skillet.

LAMB ALLA MONTECATINI

serves 6

1 Tbs butter
1 Tbs olive oil
2 lbs boned shoulder of
lamb, cut into 1½" cubes
Salt and pepper to taste
1 tsp flour
3 Tbs dry white wine
2 tsp fennel seeds
½ tsp rosemary
4 anchovy fillets,
well drained
3 cloves garlic, minced
1 cup veal or
chicken broth

In a large skillet heat butter and oil. Add the lamb cubes and brown on all sides, stirring often. Add salt and pepper. Remove lamb to a platter with a slotted spoon.

Mix flour and wine and add to the skillet. Set aside.

In a mortar and pestle, mash together fennel seeds, rosemary, anchovy fillets and garlic. Add the mixture to the skillet and mix well with wine and pan juices. Cook for 2–3 minutes.

Add lamb cubes and the broth. Cover and cook over low heat for about 1 hour or until lamb is very tender.

Serve with pan juices and your favorite pasta.

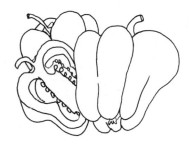

SAUCES

POMMAROLA *Basic Tomato Sauce*

10 lbs very ripe fresh
tomatoes or 2 2-lb cans
peeled Italian plum
tomatoes
2 cloves garlic,
finely chopped
2 Tbs light olive oil
1 tsp salt
½ tsp black pepper
1 Tbs minced fresh basil
or 2 tsp dry basil

Peel and seed fresh tomatoes*. Then dice. If using canned tomatoes, press through a sieve.

Put garlic in a saucepan with olive oil and simmer over low heat until garlic is light brown. Remove garlic with a slotted spoon and discard.

Swiftly pour tomatoes into the saucepan. Add salt, pepper and basil and cook over low heat, stirring frequently with a wooden spoon, until well blended.

Continue to cook and stir, uncovered, until most of the water has evaporated and sauce has thickened, about 30–40 minutes.

*NOTE: Peeling instructions page 47. To seed tomatoes: cut each tomato in half. Squeeze out seeds firmly and discard them.

**NOTE: Use 2 cups sauce for 6 servings of pasta. Remaining sauce can be refrigerated for 3–4 days, or frozen in a container with a tight lid.

TOMATO AND BASIL SAUCE FOR LINGUINE

serves 8

3 Tbs light olive oil
2 medium onions, chopped
2 garlic cloves, minced
1 28-oz can tomatoes chopped,
or
2½ lbs fresh tomatoes,
chopped
¼ cup fresh basil, minced,
or 1 Tbs dry basil
1½ tsp fresh oregano
or ½ tsp dry oregano
Salt and pepper to taste
1 lb cooked linguine
Grated Parmesan cheese

Heat oil in large skillet. Add onions and sauté until transparent, about 8 minutes. Add garlic and cook an additional 2 minutes.

Add tomatoes and herbs. Increase heat, bring to boil and cook until some of liquid has been reduced. Add salt and pepper to taste.

Pour over pasta and toss lightly. Serve immediately, sprinkled with Parmesan cheese.

BÉCHAMEL SAUCE *White Sauce*

makes about 1½ cups

1½ Tbs margarine
1½ Tbs flour
1½ cups skim or
low-fat milk
Salt and pepper to taste

Melt the margarine in a small saucepan. Remove from heat and add flour, stirring with a wooden spoon. Add the milk slowly, while continuing to stir.

Return to heat and, stirring constantly, cook until the sauce has thickened. Season with salt and pepper.

CHEESE SAUCE

makes about 1½ cups

1½ Tbs margarine
1½ Tbs flour
1½ cups skim or
low-fat milk
4 Tbs grated Swiss
or Gruyère cheese
2 Tbs grated
Parmesan cheese
½ tsp mustard
Salt and pepper to taste

Melt margarine in a saucepan. Remove from heat and add flour, stirring with a wooden spoon.

Return to heat and add milk slowly, stirring constantly until the sauce is thickened.

Add remaining ingredients and cook until cheese has melted. Add salt and pepper to taste.

LEMON SAUCE

makes about 1½ cups

Juice of 1 lemon
1 Tbs cornstarch
1½ cups dry white wine
1 Tbs margarine
1 tsp grated lemon rind

Blend lemon juice and cornstarch in a bowl. Add wine and mix until smooth.

In a small saucepan melt the margarine and add lemon-wine mixture. Cook over low heat, stirring constantly until the sauce has thickened slightly. Add the grated lemon rind.

Serve with fish, veal, or chicken.

TOMATO SAUCE

makes about 3 cups

3 Tbs light olive oil
3 Tbs minced onion
3 Tbs minced green pepper
½ cup sliced mushrooms
2 cups chopped tomatoes
½ tsp salt or more to taste
⅛ tsp pepper
2–3 drops Tabasco sauce
½ tsp basil
½ tsp oregano
½ tsp thyme

In a saucepan heat oil and cook onion, green pepper, and mushrooms over low heat for about 6 minutes. Add tomatoes and seasonings and continue cooking until the sauce is thick, about 45 minutes.

TOMATO–WINE SAUCE

makes about 2 cups

4 medium tomatoes, peeled* and chopped
1 onion, chopped
1 bay leaf
⅔ cup white wine
2 Tbs margarine
2 Tbs flour
1 tsp sugar
¼ tsp oregano
¼ tsp basil
2 Tbs tomato paste
Salt and pepper to taste

In a saucepan cook the tomatoes, onion, bay leaf, and wine for 35 minutes.

Remove the bay leaf and pour the mixture into a blender. Blend for 10 seconds.

In a saucepan melt the margarine, add flour, and cook for a minute, stirring continuously. Add the tomato mixture and stir until thickened. Add the sugar, oregano, basil, and tomato paste. Continue cooking for 5–10 minutes until sauce has thickened. Add salt and pepper to taste.

Serve over pasta or with broiled chicken or fish.

*NOTE: Peeling instructions (page 47).

serves 6–8

SALSA DI SCAMPI *Scampi Sauce*

2 Tbs oil
2 Tbs minced garlic
2 lbs fresh medium shrimp, shelled and deveined
½ cup dry white vermouth
½ cup tomato sauce
1 cup milk
½ tsp basil
½ tsp oregano
1 egg yolk
Salt and pepper
2 Tbs finely minced parsley

Heat oil in skillet. Add garlic and cook, stirring constantly for about 1 minute. Add shrimp and cook over medium heat, stirring often, until shrimp are pink.

Add vermouth and tomato sauce and cook for 1 minute. Add ¾ cup milk, the basil, and oregano.

Beat egg yolk with remaining ¼ cup milk and add to the sauce, stirring over medium heat until sauce thickens. Do not let it boil.

Season with salt and pepper to taste and pour over hot pasta. Sprinkle with parsley.

makes about 5 cups

BOLOGNESE SAUCE
This light version is especially marvelous served over ziti or rigatoni.

2 slices bacon, chopped
1 Tbs butter
3 Tbs chopped prosciutto
1 medium onion, chopped
2 carrots, finely chopped
2 celery stalks, chopped
½ lb lean beef, ground
½ lb veal, ground
¼ lb lean pork, ground
1 cup chicken broth
1 cup dry white wine
3 ripe tomatoes, peeled*
and diced or 2 cups
canned Italian plum
tomatoes, chopped
1 tsp salt
Black pepper to taste
1 clove
¼ tsp grated nutmeg
1 cup hot water
½ lb mushrooms, sliced
½ cup light cream

In a large pot cook bacon in butter until soft; add prosciutto and simmer 4 minutes. Add onion, carrots, celery and cook until soft, about 10 minutes.

Add beef, veal, and pork; stir until all red has disappeared and meat is broken up into small pieces. Add broth and wine and cook until sauce thickens, stirring constantly.

Add the tomatoes. If canned, press through a sieve. Add salt, pepper, clove, nutmeg and stir well. Taste for seasoning. Add hot water, cover pan, and simmer over low heat for 1 hour, stirring frequently.

Add mushrooms and cook, uncovered, for 10 minutes.

Just before serving sauce add cream.

Stir well, bring to boil once, take off heat and serve.

*NOTE: Peeling instructions (page 47). For keeping leftover sauce see page 109.

serves 8   # SALSA GIARDINIERA *Garden Sauce*

1 Tbs butter
1 Tbs olive oil
½ cup minced parsley
2 garlic cloves, minced
2 medium onions, minced
5 slices prosciutto,
minced
3 radishes, minced
2 carrots, minced
2 Tbs minced scallions
½ cup fresh basil
leaves, minced or 2 tsp
dry basil
4 tomatoes, diced
2 small zucchini, diced
1 cup chicken broth
Salt and pepper to taste
Romano cheese, grated

Heat butter and oil in a large pot. Add parsley, garlic, onions, prosciutto, radishes, carrots, scallions and basil. Simmer until onions and carrots are tender, about ten minutes.

Add tomatoes, zucchini, chicken broth, and salt and pepper. Simmer, covered, for 25 minutes.

Serve over hot pasta with grated cheese on the side.

about 4 cups   # SALSA D'ARAGOSTA ROSSA *Red Lobster Sauce*

2 Tbs olive oil
12 oz raw lobster meat,
cut into chunks
(lobster tails may be used)
8 oz clam juice
1 onion, peeled
1 celery stalk
3 cups Marinara Sauce
(page 114)

Heat oil in a skillet and add lobster. Cook over medium heat for about 10 minutes, turning often. Add clam juice, onion, and celery. Cover pan and simmer for 10 minutes.

Remove onion and celery from the pan and discard. Add Marinara Sauce. Stir well and simmer, uncovered, for 20 minutes, until sauce has thickened.

Serve on linguine.

*NOTE: For keeping remaining sauce, see page 109.

POMMAROLA NAPOLITANA
Neapolitan Tomato Sauce

5 Tbs minced prosciutto
2 Tbs olive oil
3 large white onions, chopped
1 Tbs fresh basil, minced or 2 tsp dry basil
12 large ripe tomatoes, peeled* and diced or 2 2-lb 3-oz cans Italian plum tomatoes
Salt and black pepper to taste

In a large saucepan sauté prosciutto in oil until crisp, but not too brown. Add onions and basil. Simmer for 5 minutes.

Add tomatoes and stir well with a wooden spoon; simmer for 25 minutes, stirring frequently.

Add salt and pepper to taste. Cook on high heat for 6–7 minutes or until water has cooked out.

*NOTE: Peeling instructions (page 47).

SALSA MARINARA *Marinara Sauce*

2 Tbs olive oil
1 medium onion, chopped
2 carrots, chopped
2 garlic cloves, minced
½ tsp black pepper
20 very ripe medium plum tomatoes, peeled*, seeded and chopped or 2 2-lb 3-oz cans Italian plum tomatoes
1 tsp salt
1 Tbs butter

Heat the oil in a saucepan. Add the onion, carrots, and garlic and sauté until onion is soft, about 5–6 minutes. Add pepper, tomatoes, and salt. Stir the sauce and cook, uncovered, for 25 minutes.

Press sauce through a sieve. Melt butter in a pot and add the strained sauce. Cook for 15 minutes, stirring frequently.

*NOTE: Peeling instructions (page 47). Seeding instructions (page 109).

**NOTE: Use 2 cups sauce for 6 servings of pasta. To keep remaining sauce, see page 109.

serves 6

SALSA TONNATA *Tuna Sauce*

1 Tbs butter
2 7-oz cans tuna
(packed in water),
drained
1 Tbs lemon juice
⅛ tsp pepper
2 Tbs parsley, minced
1 cup low-fat
evaporated milk
½ cup chicken broth
Salt and pepper to taste
2 Tbs capers, drained
and chopped

Heat butter in a skillet. Add tuna, flaking it with a fork. Heat for 7 minutes.

Add lemon juice, pepper, parsley, milk, and broth. Add salt and pepper to taste. Cook over low heat for 5 minutes. Do not let it boil.

Add capers and serve over hot pasta.

serves 6

SALSA BOLOGNESE PER TAGLIATELLE *Bolognese Sauce for Tagliatelle*

1 onion, chopped
2 carrots, diced
2 stalks celery, diced
1 green pepper, diced
3 Tbs water
2 Tbs dry vermouth
1 lb lean ground beef
16 oz prepared tomato sauce
2 cloves garlic, minced
1 bay leaf
1 cup beef broth
½ tsp salt
¼ tsp pepper
3 Tbs minced parsley
*¾ lb *tagliatelle*
(store-bought or homemade)
¼ cup grated Parmesan
cheese

In a large skillet cook onion, carrots, celery, and green pepper in water and vermouth until the onion is translucent, about 7 minutes. Remove the vegetables with a slotted spoon and set aside.

Brown the ground beef in the same pan; add more vermouth or water, if necessary, to prevent sticking. Drain the ground beef.

Add the vegetables, tomato sauce, garlic, bay leaf, broth, salt, and pepper. Simmer, uncovered, for 35 minutes, stirring occasionally. Add parsley.

Cook pasta according to package directions. Drain well.

Place pasta in a hot serving dish, pour sauce into the center, sprinkle with Parmesan cheese and serve.

*NOTE: If you wish to make your own *tagliatelle,* use Pasta Fresca recipe (page 132).

SALSA NAPOLITANA *Neapolitan Sauce*

2 Tbs light olive oil
2 cloves garlic, mashed
1 medium onion,
  finely chopped
1 green pepper,
  finely chopped
2 stalks celery,
  finely chopped
5 ripe tomatoes, chopped
½ tsp salt
  or more to taste
¼ tsp red pepper flakes
½ cup red wine

In a large skillet heat oil; add garlic, onion, green pepper, and celery and cook until vegetables are limp, but not brown.

Add tomatoes, salt, and red pepper flakes. Cook, stirring occasionally, for 5 minutes. Add wine, stir and cook, covered, over low heat for 10 minutes.

Uncover, and cook, stirring occasionally, for 10 minutes. Taste for seasoning.

Serve over your favorite pasta or over pizza.

serves 6

SALSA CON LE VONGOLE *White Clam Sauce*

1 small onion, minced
2 cloves garlic, minced
½ cup clam broth
  or chicken broth
2½ cups finely chopped
fresh clams (canned clams
  may be used)
1 cup dry white wine
1 Tbs butter
2 Tbs flour
¼ tsp oregano
¼ tsp basil
Salt and pepper to taste
1 lb spaghetti, freshly
  cooked
3 Tbs minced parsley
Grated Parmesan cheese

Place onion, garlic, and clam broth into a saucepan. Cook, stirring occasionally, until onions are very tender, about 7 minutes. Add clams and wine and cook 3–4 minutes.

Knead butter and flour together, add to clam mixture. Add oregano, basil, salt and pepper to taste. Cook over low heat, stirring constantly, until sauce has thickened.

Place spaghetti on a heated platter, cover with sauce and sprinkle with parsley. Toss lightly and serve with grated Parmesan on the side.

SALSA ROSSA DI VONGOLE *Red Clam Sauce*

serves 6

2 Tbs light olive oil
1 large onion, minced
3 cloves garlic, minced
3 Tbs minced parsley
3 cups canned Italian plum tomatoes, pureed in a blender and strained
½ cup clam juice
1 tsp basil
½ tsp sage
Salt to taste
⅛–¼ tsp red pepper flakes
1 tsp sugar
2½ cups minced clams
1 lb spaghetti or linguini, freshly cooked
Parmesan cheese

In a large skillet heat oil. Add onion and garlic and cook, stirring occasionally, until onion is tender, about 5–8 minutes.

Add parsley, tomatoes, clam juice, seasonings, and sugar. Stir well and cook over low heat for about 45 minutes or until thickened.

Add clams, bring to boil, reduce heat and simmer for 5 minutes.

Place spaghetti onto a heated platter. Pour on the sauce and toss lightly. Serve immediately with Parmesan cheese on the side.

SALSA CON SALSICCE *Sauce with Sausages*

serves 6–8

3½ oz dried mushrooms
2 cups warm water
1 large onion, minced
⅔ cup white wine
1 lb sweet Italian sausage, cut into ½″ slices
2 Tbs tomato paste
2 cups canned tomatoes, minced and puree by pressing through a sieve
Salt and pepper to taste
1 cup hot chicken broth

Place mushrooms in warm water and let soak 30 minutes. Drain well.

In a skillet combine onion and ⅓ cup wine. Cook over low heat until onion is tender and wine has almost evaporated. Add sausage and cook over low heat, stirring occasionally, for 10 minutes. Add tomato paste, tomato puree, salt and pepper. Stir lightly and cook for 5 minutes.

Chop the soaked mushrooms and add to the sausage. Add the hot broth and the remaining wine. Stir lightly, cover and simmer for about 25 minutes until sauce has thickened.

Cool the sauce and refrigerate for 3–4 hours or overnight. Remove the fat that has solidified on top of the sauce.

Reheat sauce and serve over your favorite pasta or use as a pizza sauce.

serves 6–7 # SALSA ALLA CARBONARA *Bacon and Egg Sauce*

2 strips bacon, diced
½ cup diced ham
2 cloves garlic, minced
¼ tsp red pepper flakes
Salt to taste
2 eggs, well beaten
¼ cup Parmesan cheese
1 lb spaghetti, freshly cooked

Place bacon, ham, and garlic in a saucepan and cook over low heat for 10–12 minutes. Pour off most of the fat. Add red pepper and salt to taste.

Beat eggs with Parmesan cheese.

Place freshly cooked, very hot spaghetti onto a heated platter. Add the bacon-ham mixture and the eggs and toss quickly but thoroughly.

Serve immediately with a pepper mill on the side.

*(Pasta
e Risotti)*

PASTA
AND RICE

ROTOLE DI PASTA RIPIENO *Filled Pasta Roll*

1 recipe Soft Pasta
(following)
2 10-oz pkgs frozen
chopped spinach, thawed
and squeezed dry
½ lb low-fat
ricotta cheese
2 eggs
¾ cup grated
Parmesan cheese
⅛ tsp nutmeg
Salt and pepper to taste
Boiling water, salted
1½ cups Béchamel Sauce
(page 110)

Roll pasta very thin on a heavily floured board into a 14″ × 18″ rectangle. Cut in half, horizontally, and let dry 10 minutes.

In a bowl combine spinach, ricotta, eggs, ½ cup of the Parmesan cheese, nutmeg, salt and pepper.

Place the 2 rolled-out sheets of dough into a very large pot of boiling water. Cook pasta 60 seconds or until barely tender. Place into a large roasting pan filled with cold water for 2–3 minutes. Carefully remove pasta from water with your hands and place on a damp cloth. Do not worry if pasta tears; it will be covered with sauce. Let dry 15 minutes.

Prepare Béchamel Sauce: And preheat oven to 350°.

Place ½ the spinach-ricotta mixture on the edge of a sheet of pasta and roll jelly-roll fashion. Place the remaining mixture on the edge of the second sheet of pasta and roll up. Place the 2 rolls into an oiled baking pan.

Mix Béchamel Sauce and remaining Parmesan; pour over the rolls. Bake 20–25 minutes until lightly browned.

Loosen bottom of rolls with a broad spatula. Let rest in a warm place 5 minutes before slicing. To serve, slice diagonally with a very sharp knife.

SOFT PASTA

Food Processor Method:

1 cup flour
2 eggs
2 Tbs oil
1 Tbs white wine
¼ tsp salt

Place all the ingredients into a food processor. Blend thoroughly. If the dough feels sticky, add 1–3 tablespoons flour.

Place dough on well-floured board and knead until smooth, about 1 minute. This dough is much softer than regular pasta. Let rest for 45 minutes, covered with a bowl, before rolling out.

Conventional Method:

Place all ingredients into a bowl and knead by hand until the dough holds together, about 3 minutes. Add 1–3 tablespoons more flour if dough feels sticky.

Place the dough onto a well-floured board and knead until smooth, about 2–3 minutes. Let rest for 45 minutes, covered with a bowl, before rolling out.

PESTO ALLA GENOVESE *Pesto Genoa Style*

serves 6–8

*1 cup fresh basil leaves, minced
1 cup fresh Italian parsley, minced
½ cup grated Parmesan cheese
½ cup grated Romano cheese
**8 blanched almonds
2 Tbs pignoli nuts
**10 blanched walnut halves
3 garlic cloves
4 Tbs olive oil
1 lb *fettuccine*
(store-bought or homemade)

Place all ingredients except *fettuccine* in the blender and blend into a smooth paste (*pesto*). Place the *pesto* on a large warm platter.

Cook *fettuccine* as directed on the package. Drain well. Reserve ½ cup of the cooking liquid.

Place pasta on the platter with the *pesto* and toss well. Add the hot reserved cooking liquid and toss again.

Serve immediately in hot soup bowls.

*NOTE: The real *pesto* is made only with fresh basil leaves, but when they are not available, you can substitute fresh spinach leaves for basil. Use 1 tablespoon dry basil and 1 cup minced fresh spinach leaves.

NOTE: To blanch almonds and walnuts: drop into boiling water, remove from heat and let stand 10 minutes. Remove skins.

FETTUCINE FIORENTINA *Noodles Florentine*

serves 8

1 lb green *fettucine* (store-bought)
1 Tbs margarine
2 cups low-fat ricotta cheese
2 10-oz pkgs chopped frozen spinach, defrosted
1½ cups Béchamel Sauce (page 110)
½ cup grated Parmesan cheese
½ tsp salt
¼ tsp white pepper
½ tsp Italian seasoning

Cook *fettucine* as directed on package. Drain well and toss with the margarine.

Butter an oblong (8″ × 16″) or square dish. Spread ½ the noodles evenly in bottom of dish. Spread ricotta over the noodles.

Squeeze out as much water as possible from the spinach; spread spinach over the noodles. Pour ½ the Béchamel Sauce over the spinach; sprinkle with Parmesan cheese, salt and pepper, and Italian seasoning. Spread another layer of noodles and pour remaining Béchamel over the noodles.

Bake in a preheated 350° oven for 25–30 minutes or until slightly browned on top.

CRESPELLE FIORENTINA *Crepes*
Florentine

1 Tbs butter
2 Tbs minced scallions
(white parts only)
1 cup minced fresh
mushrooms
1 cup low-fat ricotta
cheese at room temperature
1 egg
2 cups Béchamel Sauce
(following)
1½ cups chopped spinach
(fresh or frozen),
thoroughly drained
20 6-in crepes (page 128)
¼ cup grated
Parmesan cheese

Heat butter in a 10″ skillet. Add scallions and sauté until just transparent. Add mushrooms and sauté until moisture has evaporated. Add ricotta cheese, egg, and 4 tablespoons Béchamel Sauce to make a thick paste. Set aside.

Mix ⅓ cup remaining sauce with spinach.

Place a crepe in bottom of a lightly oiled baking dish. Spread with spinach mixture, cover with another crepe and spread with layer of mushroom-cheese mixture. Repeat, alternating crepes and fillings, finishing with a crepe. Pour rest of sauce over crepes and sprinkle with grated Parmesan.

Refrigerate 2 hours before baking. Bake in a preheated 375° oven about 30–35 minutes until bubbling hot, with cheese lightly browned.

BÉCHAMEL SAUCE
2 Tbs butter
2 Tbs all-purpose flour
2 cups low-fat
milk, at room temperature
2 Tbs freshly grated
Parmesan cheese

Melt butter in saucepan. When butter foams, add flour and mix well. Remove from heat; slowly add milk, mixing with whisk until smooth.

Stirring constantly, return to heat and simmer 5 minutes. Remove from heat and add Parmesan. Makes 2 cups.

VERMICELLI CON LE COZZE *Vermicelli with Tomato and Mussel Sauce*

1½ qts fresh mussels
1 cup water
2 Tbs olive oil
1 medium onion,
finely chopped
3 cloves garlic, minced
3 cups chopped tomatoes
(fresh or canned)

Wash and debeard mussels. Discard those that do not close tightly when sharply tapped.

Put mussels in a large pot with the water and cook 5–6 minutes or until the shells open. Remove from heat and drain. Set aside a few of the mussels in their shells to garnish. Shell the rest of the mussels.

¾ lb vermicelli
(store-bought or homemade)
Salt and pepper
2 Tbs chopped
fresh parsley

Heat oil in a large skillet and sauté the onion until golden. Add garlic and tomatoes. Simmer for about 35 minutes.

Cook vermicelli as directed on package. Drain thoroughly and place on a heated platter.

Add salt and pepper and the mussels to the sauce and bring to boil. Pour the sauce on top of pasta.

Serve immediately, garnished with the reserved mussels and chopped parsley.

PASTA WITH FRESH TOMATOES AND HERBS

serves 6

2 lbs very ripe tomatoes,
chopped very fine
5 cloves garlic, mashed
3 Tbs olive oil
Salt and pepper to taste
1 tsp minced fresh
basil or ¼ tsp dry
1 tsp minced fresh sage
or ¼ tsp dry
1 lb pasta shells
(store-bought)

Place chopped tomatoes and garlic into a chilled bowl. Pour the oil over tomatoes; add salt, pepper, and the herbs. Toss lightly. Cover the bowl with plastic and refrigerate for at least 3 hours before serving.

Cook the pasta as directed on the package. It should be *al dente*, not overcooked.

Drain the pasta and immediately place in a heated bowl or on 6 heated plates. Pour on the sauce and toss well. The pasta must be very hot when the ice-cold sauce is poured on top—that is the secret to the taste of this marvelous dish.

RAVIOLI VERDI *Green Ravioli with Cheese*

1 recipe Pasta Verde
(page 127)
4 qts water and
1 Tbs salt
3–4 Tbs melted butter
½–⅔ cup freshly grated
Parmesan cheese

In a bowl mix together ricotta, Parmesan and Gruyère cheeses. Add the egg, salt, pepper, and sage and mix well. Cover bowl with plastic and refrigerate for 3–4 hours.

To Make Up Ravioli:

FILLING

2 cups low-fat ricotta
½ cup freshly grated
Parmesan cheese
½ cup grated
Gruyère cheese
1 beaten egg
Salt and white pepper
to taste
¼ tsp dry sage
or 1 tsp chopped fresh sage

Roll out ½ the dough to a ¼" thickness, about 36" square (18" on each side). Cut the square into 2 equal strips.

With a teaspoon place small mounds of filling about 2" apart, in even rows, on 1 of the strips.

Moisten the dough between the mounds with a little water, using your fingers or a pastry brush. Cover the mounds with the second strip of dough. Press the top sheet very firmly around each mound of filling.

Cut the dough into ravioli, each about 2" square. Be sure that each ravioli square is firmly closed.

Roll out, cut and fill the remaining dough in the same fashion. Cover the ravioli and let them dry for 30–45 minutes.

To Cook Ravioli:

Bring salted water to boil in a large pot.

Drop 14–16 pieces of ravioli into the pot and cook over low heat for 8–10 minutes. Remove ravioli with a slotted spoon and place on a heated platter. Pour a little melted butter over them.

Continue cooking ravioli and placing them on the platter. Pour remaining melted butter over them and sprinkle with grated cheese.

Serve immediately.

*NOTE: The ravioli may be made from red pasta or your favorite white pasta. If you have a Ravioli Chef, by all means use it.

PASTA VERDE *Tuscan Green Pasta*

3 oz fresh spinach leaves
with stems removed
2 qts water and
1 Tbs salt
3½ cups all-purpose
unbleached flour
2 eggs
2½ tsp vegetable oil
¼ tsp salt
⅛ tsp finely ground
white pepper
1–3 Tbs water,
as needed

Wash spinach leaves and drain. In a large pot bring salted water to boil and add the spinach. Reduce heat and simmer for about 10 minutes.

Drain spinach in a colander; then place colander with spinach under cold running water for 2–3 minutes. Squeeze spinach dry. Mince spinach and measure out 3 level tablespoonfuls. Reserve rest for another time.

Place flour in a mound on a pastry board and make a well in the center. Break eggs into the well; add oil, salt, pepper, and the 3 tablespoons of spinach.

Mix together eggs, oil, and spinach with a fork, scooping up a bit of flour. With your fingers start blending flour with the egg mixture, always bringing up fresh flour from the outer rim and turning the mixed dough under the flour.

When most of the flour has been absorbed, start kneading dough with the palms of your hands until it is smooth and elastic. Add water if needed.

Turn the dough out onto a lightly floured board and knead 2 minutes. Shape into a ball, cover with a towel and let rest 15–20 minutes before rolling out and either cutting or putting through a pasta machine.

Let dough dry an additional 15 minutes before cooking. You may make *fettuccine*, *linguine*, *cannelloni* or *tagliatelle*.

*NOTE: If you wish, make the dough in a food processor. Insert metal knife into the processor.

Blend all ingredients, except water. Blend until a ball of dough forms, about 30–40 seconds. If dough does not form, add a little water by teaspoonfuls until dough holds together.

Turn out onto a lightly floured board and knead for 1 minute. Shape into a ball, cover with a towel and let rest 15–20 minutes. Then proceed as above.

PASTA ROSSA   *Red Pasta*

2–3 canned red beets,
minced
3½ cups all-purpose
unbleached flour
2 eggs
2½ tsp vegetable oil
½ tsp salt
⅛ tsp finely ground
white pepper
1–3 Tbs water,
as needed

Mash beets into a paste and measure out 3 table-spoonfuls.

Then, using remaining ingredients, follow directions for making Pasta Verde (page 127), substituting the beets for the spinach.

serves 6–8 # MANICOTTI FIORENTINA *Crepes with Spinach and Cheese Filling*

BASIC CREPE BATTER
3 eggs
1 cup all-purpose
flour, sifted
⅛ tsp salt
1 cup low-fat milk
½ cup water
2 Tbs melted butter

In a blender combine eggs, flour, salt, milk, and water. Blend for a few seconds. Add butter, scrape down the sides of blender, then blend again until very smooth. Let stand for 1 hour covered.

Use a 5″ or 6″ non-stick crepe pan. To test for heat: drop a bit of batter onto pan; if it browns quickly, pan is hot enough.

Pour 2–3 tablespoons batter into pan and tilt pan left and right so that the batter covers the bottom evenly. This should be just a thin film of batter; pour off any excess. Brown slightly on 1 side, turn with a spatula and brown the other side.

Stack crepes on a platter. Makes about 16 6″ crepes.

FILLING
1 lb low-fat
ricotta cheese
½ cup low-fat
grated mozzarella cheese
½ cup ground
Parmesan cheese
½ tsp salt or
more if needed
¼ tsp Italian seasoning
¼ tsp white pepper

Make up filling by combining the cheeses, seasonings, and garlic. Blend well.

Squeeze out all the moisture from the spinach. Add to cheeses and blend again. Taste for seasoning.

Spread about ½ cup Pommarola in a square or oblong baking pan, 8″ × 16″. Place about 1 or 2 tablespoons ricotta mixture on each crepe and roll up. Do not tuck

1 clove garlic, crushed
(optional)
2 10-oz pkgs frozen chopped
spinach, defrosted and
well drained
2 cups Basic Tomato Sauce,
(page 109)

TOPPING
2 cups Béchamel Sauce (page
110)
½ cup grated
Parmesan cheese
Salt and pepper

in ends. Place rolled up crepes side by side in the baking dish and top with remaining tomato sauce. Pour Béchamel Sauce over the Manicotti. Sprinkle with Parmesan cheese and bake in a 375° oven for 20 minutes. Serve immediately.

You may assemble the Manicotti the day before. Place into the baking dish. Do not top with either of the sauces or cheese. Refrigerate.

Just before baking, top with Pommarola and Béchamel Sauce. Bake and serve immediately.

*NOTE: When using this Béchamel recipe, increase ingredient amounts proportionately to make 2 cups.

serves 8

RAVIOLI NUDI   *Spinach Dumplings*

3 10-oz pkgs frozen chopped
spinach, thawed and
well drained
1 lb low-fat
ricotta cheese
3 egg yolks
1 cup finely grated
Parmesan cheese
½ tsp nutmeg
2 cloves garlic, mashed
Salt and pepper to taste
1 cup flour
8 cups water and
1 Tbs salt
4 Tbs melted butter

Cook spinach for 2–3 minutes and cool; squeeze dry.

Mix spinach, ricotta, yolks, ½ cup Parmesan cheese, nutmeg, garlic, salt and pepper. Blend well. Shape into 1″ balls and roll in flour.

Place on a cookie sheet, but don't let the balls touch each other. Place 5–6 balls at a time into simmering salted water. As the balls rise to the top, remove with a slotted spoon.

Place in an ovenproof serving dish with the melted butter. Gently roll balls to coat them with butter.

Sprinkle with remaining ½ cup Parmesan cheese, cover and heat in a 350° oven for 5 minutes. Serve immediately.

PASTA FOR RAVIOLI, RAVIOLINI, AGNOLOTTI, AND TORTELLINI

4 cups all-purpose unbleached flour or Semolina flour, if available
1½ tsp salt
3 eggs
1½ Tbs light olive oil
2–3 Tbs warm water

Place salt and flour into a large bowl. Make a well in the center. Break eggs into the well and add oil.

Knead lightly, adding water as needed to make a soft dough. Knead for about 2 minutes in the bowl.

Turn out onto a lightly floured board and knead for an additional 5–6 minutes or until the dough is very smooth. Shape into a ball, cover with an inverted bowl and let rest for 30 minutes.

To Make Dough in Food Processor:

Insert steel blade into the processor. Blend all ingredients except water.

Blend in fast, short bursts until dough begins sticking together, adding hot water, as needed, by teaspoonfuls. Add just enough water to form a ball of soft dough.

Turn out onto a floured board and knead by hand for 2–3 minutes or until very smooth. Shape into a ball, cover with an inverted bowl and let rest for 30 minutes.

To Shape and Fill Ravioli or Raviolini:

See Ravioli Verdi (page 126).

To Shape and Fill Agnolotti:

Divide dough into 2 parts. Leave 1 part under the bowl. Roll out the other part on a lightly floured board as thin as possible.

Cut into circles with a 2″ plain or fluted cookie cutter. Immediately place about 1 teaspoon filling into the center of the circle. Fold over to form a half-moon. Press the edges firmly together.

If the dough does not stick, brush inside edges with a bit of water then pinch firmly together.

Roll out reserved dough, cut into circles and proceed as above.

To Shape and Fill Tortellini:

Divide, roll out dough and cut into 2″ circles as directed for *agnolotti* (above). Place filling in center, shape into half-moons. Seal well.

Bend the half-moon, seam side out, forming a ring. Pinch the ends firmly together.

FILLINGS FOR RAVIOLI, AGNOLOTTI, TORTELLINI*

FILLING MADE FROM LEFTOVERS
makes about 36 ravioli, 36 agnolotti, 48 tortellini

½ lb leftover ground chicken, veal, or ham
1 egg, lightly beaten
3 Tbs grated Parmesan cheese
⅛ tsp nutmeg
2 Tbs milk
Salt and pepper to taste

In a bowl blend all the ingredients into a smooth paste, and stuff the ravioli, *agnolotti* or *tortellini*.

*NOTE: If you wish, use the Ravioli Verdi filling (p. 126) as another option.

CHEESE AND SPINACH FILLING

See Manicotti (page 128); Pommarola sauce is not part of filling but may be used as a sauce.

CHEESE FILLING
1 cup low-fat ricotta
¼ cup grated Romano cheese
¼ cup grated Parmesan cheese
½ cup grated Swiss or Gruyère cheese
2 egg yolks, well beaten
1 Tbs minced scallions
1 Tbs minced parsley
Salt and pepper to taste

In a bowl blend all ingredients and use as filling.

Place filled ravioli, *raviolini*, *agnolotti*, or *tortellini* onto a kitchen towel, cover with another towel and let stand for 30 minutes before boiling.

Cook ravioli, *agnolotti* or *tortellini* as directed for Ravioli Verdi (page 126).

Serve with your favorite tomato sauce or sprinkle with melted butter and Parmesan cheese. Or cook in chicken broth and serve as directed for Raviolini in Brodo (page 44).

serves 8–10 # PASTA FRESCA *Fresh Pasta Dough*

For Fettuccine, Cannelloni, Linguine, Lasagna, Taglia-telle, Ravioli, Raviolini, and many other pastas.

4 cups all-purpose
unbleached flour or
Semolina
flour, if available
4 eggs, lightly beaten
1 tsp salt
2 Tbs light olive oil
1–2 Tbs warm water

Follow directions for making dough for Ravioli and other pastas (page 130).

To Roll Out and Cut the Dough:

Divide the ball of dough into 3 parts. Roll out each part on a lightly floured board as thin as possible using a straight rolling pin, 2″ in diameter.

Dust rolled-out dough lightly with flour and brush with a wide pastry brush to distribute flour evenly. Roll up the dough into loose roll, 2½″–3″ in diameter.

For *tagliatelle*, cut into strips ¾″ wide; *cannelloni* into 4″ × 4″ squares; *lasagna* into 3″ × 6″ strips; *fettuccine* into strips, ½″ wide. For *linguine*: roll the dough to a ¼″ thickness and cut into long strips, ⅛″ or ¼″ wide.

It's certainly easier and great fun to make pasta in a pasta machine: roll out dough to a ½″ thickness then put through a *lasagna*, *cannelloni*, *fettuccine*, or *linguine* roller. Follow the directions that come with the machine.

serves 4–6 # POLENTA *Cornmeal*

4¼ cups water
½–¾ tsp salt to taste
2 cups yellow cornmeal

In a 2–3 quart pot bring water and salt just to simmering point.

Start pouring in the cornmeal very slowly with one hand, while steadily stirring with your other hand. (The cornmeal lumps easily and the steady, continuous stirring breaks up the lumps.) If lumps form, break them up immediately against the sides of the pot. Cook about 30–35 minutes, stirring constantly.

Turn off heat, cover pot and let the *polenta* stand 3–4 minutes, without stirring. Shake pot a few times to loosen *polenta* from the sides.

Lightly oil a plate, place over the pot and invert pot to unmold *polenta* onto the plate. In Italy, *polenta* is customarily cut with a string, but it can be cut with a sharp knife and served in wedges or squares.

Serve with one of your favorite sauces or sprinkled with cheese

RISOTTO AL FORNO *Baked Rice*

serves 8

4 oz dried
Italian mushrooms
Hot water to cover
1 large onion,
chopped
⅓ cup dry white wine
2 cloves garlic,
minced
3 celery stalks,
minced
2 cups canned Italian
plum tomatoes, chopped
2 cups chicken broth
2 cups long grain rice
or Italian rice
2 Tbs butter
Salt and pepper to taste
⅓ cup grated
Parmesan cheese

Soak mushrooms in hot water to cover for 1 hour. Drain, chop fine and set aside.

In a pot cook onions in wine until tender and most of liquid has evaporated. Add garlic, celery, and tomatoes. Stir well and cook covered, stirring occasionally, until the liquid has cooked down and mixture has thickened.

Add mushrooms and chicken broth. Bring to boil and set aside.

Cook rice as directed on the package but shorten cooking time to 15 minutes. Drain rice and add to tomato mixture. Add the butter and salt and pepper to taste. Transfer to a lightly buttered casserole.

Bake in a 350° oven, covered, for 25 minutes or until very tender. Sprinkle Parmesan cheese on rice. Bake for 5 minutes and serve.

PIZZA CASALINGA *Homemade Pizza*

½ pkg granulated yeast
¼ cup lukewarm water
2 cups unbleached
all-purpose flour
½ tsp salt
⅓ cup lukewarm water
1–2 Tbs light olive oil

In a small bowl mix yeast and the ¼ cup water. Let stand 5 minutes.

Place flour and salt into a bowl and make a well in the center. Pour in yeast mixture and the additional ⅓ cup water. Start kneading the flour toward the center, absorbing yeast and water.

Continue kneading for 2 minutes. Add a bit more water if the dough feels dry. This should be a soft dough.

Turn dough out onto a floured board and knead for about 2 minutes or until it starts to blister. Place into a lightly oiled bowl. Cover and let rise for about 45 minutes in a warm place (on top of cooled stove) or until doubled in bulk.

While dough is rising you can prepare vegetables in Topping (below).

TOPPING #1
For 2 10″ Pizzas

3 ripe tomatoes,
thinly sliced
2 green peppers, sliced
into thin strips
12–14 large mushrooms,
thinly sliced
Salt and pepper to taste
½ tsp basil
¼ tsp oregano
1 cup low-fat grated
mozzarella cheese

When dough is ready, punch down, divide in 2 parts and shape each part into a ball.

Oil lightly 2 10″ pizza pans or 2 jelly-roll pans. Roll out the 2 balls of dough into 10″ circles, each. The circles should be thin in the center and thicker around the edges. Oil the pizza circles lightly.

On each of the pizzas, spread ½ the ingredients. Begin with a layer of tomatoes. Spread peppers on top of tomatoes and top with mushrooms. Sprinkle each layer with salt, pepper, basil, and oregano. Sprinkle cheese on top of mushrooms.

Bake in a 450° preheated oven for 10 minutes. Reduce heat to 375° and bake for 10 minutes or until the edges of pizza are lightly browned. Serve immediately.

TOPPING #2: SALSA CON SALSICCE
(Sauce with Sausages)

Use recipe on page 117. Plus 1 cup low-fat mozzarella cheese.

Roll out pizzas as directed for Topping #1. Place into oiled pans and spread sauce over lightly oiled pizzas. Sprinkle each with ½ cup mozzarella and bake as directed.

TOPPING #3: SALSA NAPOLITANA
(Neapolitan Sauce)

Use recipe on page 116. Plus 1 cup low-fat mozzarella cheese.

Follow topping and baking directions as above.

TOPPING #4: POMMAROLA
(Basic Tomato Sauce)

Use recipe on page 109. Plus 1 cup low-fat mozzarella cheese.

Follow topping and baking directions as above.

RISOTTO CON FUNGHI *Rice with Mushrooms*

2 Tbs butter
1 medium onion,
finely chopped
1 clove garlic, minced
2½ cups Italian rice
(such as Avorio) or
long grain rice
⅓ cup dry white vermouth
4½ cups boiling
chicken broth
½ lb mushrooms,
thinly sliced
⅛ tsp red pepper flakes
Salt to taste
½ cup grated
Parmesan cheese

Heat butter in a large heavy pot; add onion and garlic and cook until onion is just limp. Add rice to the onion and cook, stirring continuously, about 5–6 minutes.

Add vermouth and ½ the boiling broth. Increase heat and cook, stirring occasionally with a fork, for 2 minutes. Reduce heat to low and cook, stirring occasionally with the fork, until most of the liquid has been absorbed.

Add remaining boiling broth and cook over low heat 3–4 minutes, stirring occasionally. Cover pot and cook rice until all moisture has evaporated and the rice is tender, about 20–25 minutes.

Add mushrooms and cook, stirring occasionally, for 3–4 minutes. Add the Parmesan cheese and blend well. Cook for an additional 1 minute and serve immediately.

If desired, serve additional Parmesan cheese on the side and place a pepper mill on the table.

serves 6–8 # RISO E BROCCOLI *Rice and Broccoli*

1 head broccoli
Water and 1 tsp salt
2 Tbs light olive oil
1 medium onion,
finely chopped
2 cups Italian or
long grain rice
4 cups boiling
chicken broth
Salt and pepper to taste
2 Tbs minced parsley
⅓ cup Parmesan cheese

Cut stems off broccoli and divide into flowerettes. Cook in salted water until just tender, about 10 minutes. Drain and chop fine.

In a heavy pot heat oil and cook onion until barely golden. Add broccoli and cook until tender, about 4 minutes, stirring often with a fork. Add rice and gently stir to coat rice with the mixture.

Add boiling broth, toss rice once with the fork, bring to boil, then reduce heat. Cover and cook over low heat for about 25 minutes, or until all liquid has been absorbed and rice is tender.

Blend in the Parmesan cheese and serve immediately with additional grated cheese on the side.

serves 8   # CROCHETTE BICOLORE *Two-Color Fritters*

2½ cups minced cooked spinach, well drained (use fresh or frozen*)
2 cups cooked rice
2 eggs, beaten
½ cup grated Parmesan cheese
½ cup flour or a little more as needed
Salt and pepper to taste
⅛ tsp nutmeg
3 qts water and 1 Tbs salt
2 Tbs melted butter
Parmesan cheese

In a bowl combine spinach, rice, eggs, cheese, and ¼ cup flour. Blend lightly with a fork. If the mixture does not stick together, add a little more flour, 1 teaspoonful at a time.

Add salt, pepper and nutmeg and blend lightly. Refrigerate mixture for 1 hour.

Shape into 1″ balls and roll in the remaining ¼ cup flour. Use extra flour, if needed.

In a large pot bring water and salt to boil, reduce heat to simmer and drop about 8 rice balls at a time into the simmering water. Cook 4–5 minutes or until balls rise to the surface. Remove with a slotted spoon and drain on paper towels.

Place in a serving dish and sprinkle with butter. Keep warm in a 150° oven until all the fritters have been cooked. Serve with Parmesan cheese on the side.

*NOTE: You will need 1½ lbs fresh spinach. Wash thoroughly, then boil or steam for 6–7 minutes. Or use 2 10-oz packages frozen spinach and cook as directed on the package.

(Dolci)

DESSERTS

CASSATA MAGRA *Lean Cassata*

serves 8–10

1½ cups low-fat ricotta cheese
¼ cup sugar
1 tsp vanilla
2 pts vanilla ice milk, slightly softened
2 Tbs finely chopped candied fruit
Garnish: fresh strawberries or raspberries

In a bowl combine ricotta cheese, sugar and vanilla. Beat with an electric hand beater until smooth.

Add the ice milk and continue beating with the electric beater until well blended. Fold in the candied fruit.

Pour into a 1½ quart round or square serving dish, cover with foil and freeze until firm.

Remove from freezer, unwrap and garnish with the berries. Serve immediately.

ORANGE ZABAGLIONE

serves 8–10

7 egg yolks
1½ Tbs sugar
1½ cups orange juice

In top of a double boiler, beat yolks and sugar until thick and lemon colored. Place over hot water and slowly add orange juice, beating with a whisk until the mixture is the consistency of thick cream.

Remove from heat and pour into 8 or 10 serving dishes. Serve hot or refrigerate for 3–4 hours before serving.

CREMA DI MASCHERPONE *Cream Cheese Dessert*

serves 4

8 oz cream cheese, softened
2 eggs, separated
¼ cup sugar
2 Tbs orange liqueur, brandy, or rum
1½ cups sliced strawberries, blueberries, or sliced peaches

Press the cream cheese through a sieve into a bowl. Beat in the egg yolks, sugar, and the liqueur, beating until the mixture is smooth.

Beat egg whites until stiff but not dry and fold thoroughly into the cream. Place in a serving dish and top with fruit.

BISCUIT TORTONI

makes 12–14

2 cups low-cal whipped topping, sweetened or unsweetened, ready-made
4 Tbs rum
½ tsp rum extract
½ cup finely chopped toasted almonds
2 egg whites, stiffly beaten

In a bowl combine topping, rum, and rum extract. Fold in ¼ cup of the almonds and the egg whites.

Place in 12–14 fluted paper cupcake cups and sprinkle with remaining almonds.

Freeze for 24 hours. Serve frozen.

LEMON MOUSSE

serves 6

6 large lemons
3 egg yolks
⅓ cup sugar
4 Tbs lemon juice
Grated rind of 1 lemon
4 egg whites
¼ tsp cream of tartar

Preheat oven to 350°.

Slice ends from lemons, to level them. Cut horizontally in ½ to make 12 small lemon cups. Scoop out pulp, carefully, and discard. Do not pierce the shells. Drain shells on paper towels.

Beat yolks with 4 tablespoons sugar until thick. Add lemon juice and rind.

Beat whites with cream of tartar. Add remaining sugar and beat until stiff.

Fold whites into yolk mixture. Fill the 12 lemon cups with mixture.

Place in a baking dish and bake 16–18 minutes or until lightly browned.

ZABAGLIONE *Egg Dessert*

serves 6

6 egg yolks
5 Tbs sugar
8 Tbs Marsala wine
1/4 tsp nutmeg

Combine all ingredients except nutmeg in top of double boiler. Place over simmering water and whip with a wire whisk until thick and light in color, about 10 minutes.

Serve warm or cold, sprinkled with nutmeg.

MOUSSE CARDINALE

serves 6

2 pkgs strawberry-flavored diet gelatin
1 cup sliced fresh strawberries
1 tsp artificial sweetener
2 egg whites
2 Tbs sugar
1 cup stiffly-beaten low-cal dessert topping
Garnish: whole strawberries

Prepare gelatin as directed on the package; cool, but do not let it set.

Sprinkle strawberries with sweetener. Fold into the cooled gelatin.

Beat egg whites until stiff; add sugar and beat until very stiff. Fold into partially set gelatin, then fold in the topping. Let set completely.

Decorate with whole strawberries.

*NOTE: Other berries or fruit may be used in this recipe. Oranges, blueberries, peaches, etc. Vary gelatin flavor according to taste.

ORANGE CUSTARD WITH MANDARIN ORANGES

serves 6

1/4 cup frozen orange juice
4 eggs
2 Tbs sugar
1 1/2 cups skim or low-fat milk, scalded
1 tsp vanilla extract
1 Tbs orange rind
1 tsp artificial sweetener (optional)
1 small can mandarin oranges, drained

Beat the frozen orange juice, eggs, and sugar until light in color and slightly thickened. Add the scalded milk, beating continuously. Mix in vanilla, orange rind, and sweetener.

Pour custard into 6 custard cups. Place the cups into a shallow pan of hot water. Bake in a 350° oven for 50 minutes or until an inserted knife comes out clean.

Cool, then refrigerate. Decorate each custard with a few mandarin oranges.

RICOTTA FREEZE

1½ cups low-fat
ricotta cheese
¼ cup sugar
1 tsp vanilla
2 pts vanilla ice milk,
slightly softened
Garnish: fresh strawberries
or raspberries

Blend ricotta cheese, sugar, and vanilla in a blender until smooth. Add to ice milk and beat with an electric beater until blended.

Pour into a 5″ × 9″ loaf mold, cover with foil and freeze until firm.

To unmold, dip pan into hot water and unmold onto a platter. Garnish with berries.

serves 6 # PESCHE RIPIENE *Stuffed Baked Peaches*

2 qts water
6 large, firm,
ripe peaches
½ cup fine cake crumbs
½ cup ground hazelnuts
1 Tbs butter, softened
Juice of 1 lemon

Bring water to boil in a saucepan. Immerse peaches in boiling water for a few seconds to loosen the skins, then drain and plunge into cold water.

Peel and halve peaches and remove the stones. Using a teaspoon, scoop enough flesh from each half to make a deep indentation. Chop the scooped-out flesh.

Mix the peach flesh with cake crumbs, nuts, butter, and lemon juice. Pile the stuffing into the peach halves and smooth down the top. Arrange the peaches side by side in a shallow ovenproof baking dish.

Bake in a preheated 350° oven for 30–35 minutes. Serve hot or chilled.

serves 6–8 # MELON MÉLANGE

2 cups cantaloupe balls
2 cups honeydew balls
2 cups watermelon balls
*1 10-oz pkg frozen
raspberries, thawed,
pureed, and strained
3 Tbs raspberry liqueur
or strawberry liqueur
1 pt vanilla ice milk

In a large bowl combine melon balls, strained raspberries, and liqueur. Cover and refrigerate until ready to serve.

To serve, place a scoop of ice milk into individual serving dishes and place the melon balls with sauce on top.

*NOTE: Pureé raspberries in a blender then strain through a sieve. Discard the seeds.

serves 6 # BRANDIED PEACHES

6 fresh ripe peaches
1/3 cup peach brandy

Peel* and slice fresh peaches. Pour 1/2 the peach brandy over the peaches and refrigerate until ready to serve.

Heat the remaining brandy in a ladle or a small pot until lukewarm. Ignite and pour over the peaches.

*NOTE: *To peel peaches:* Bring 8 cups water to boil. Drop peaches into the boiling water for 30–40 seconds. Remove with a slotted spoon and peel with a small sharp knife.

serves 8 # BRANDIED STRAWBERRIES

2 pts fresh strawberries
1/4 cup sugar
1/4 cup brandy

Wash and hull the berries. Sprinkle with sugar and let stand for 30 minutes.

In a ladle or small pot, heat brandy until lukewarm. Ignite and pour over the strawberries.

serves 8 # PESCHE DOLCE *Peach Fluff*

2 1-lb cans peach halves,
packed in water
1/2 cup honey
1 1/2 pkgs. unflavored
gelatin
4 Tbs dark rum
1/3 cup fresh orange juice
4 Tbs water
1 envelope
topping mix
1/2 cup low-fat milk
4 egg whites
Pinch cream of tartar
Garnish: peach slices

Use a 2 1/2-quart soufflé dish.

Drain the peaches and reserve 3 peach halves for garnish. Puree remaining peaches with honey in the blender.

Soften gelatin in water. Heat rum and orange juice in a saucepan. Remove from heat and add gelatin. Continue stirring until gelatin is completely melted. Add to the peach puree.

Make topping mix according to package directions, using the milk. Fold into peach mixture and chill until slightly thickened.

Beat egg whites with cream of tartar until stiff. Fold into peach mixture. Pour mixture into the soufflé dish. Chill about 6 hours.

When ready to serve, garnish with the sliced peaches.

serves 6 # PERE RIPIENE *Stuffed Pears*

6 medium pears, peeled
and cut in half lengthwise
2 Tbs lemon juice
⅔ cup low-fat
ricotta cheese
½ cup crumbled
Gorgonzola cheese
¼ tsp nutmeg
½–⅔ cup ground walnuts

Hollow out each pear half. Sprinkle pears with lemon juice.

In a bowl cream ricotta, Gorgonzola, and nutmeg with a wooden spoon until well blended. Fill each pear half with the cheese mixture.

Put two halves together; smooth any cheese that seeps out with a spatula. Roll pears in ground walnuts.

Place on a serving platter, cover with foil and refrigerate 2–3 hours.

serves 6 # POACHED PEARS

6 whole pears, peeled
12 cloves
2½ cups red wine
(Burgundy)
1 Tbs honey
1 Tbs sugar
¼ tsp nutmeg
¼ tsp cinnamon

Stick each pear with 2 cloves. Place in a saucepan.

Add wine, honey, sugar, nutmeg and cinnamon. Bring to boil. Cover, reduce heat and cook 15–20 minutes or until pears are barely tender.

Let the pears cool in the wine turning them occasionally. Served chilled.

serves 10–12 # CHERRY AND APRICOT CAKE MERANO

4 Tbs light brown sugar
1 Tbs melted butter
2 tsp lemon juice
¼ tsp allspice
½ tsp cinnamon
1 16-oz can apricot
halves, packed in water
½ cup pitted red
cherries, packed in water
1½ cups sifted flour
2 tsp baking powder
⅛ tsp salt
2 eggs, separated
½ cup sugar
6 Tbs hot water
*3–4 Tbs powdered vanilla
sugar—optional

Preheat oven to 350°. Oil lightly a 9″ cake pan.

Mix brown sugar, melted butter, lemon juice, allspice, and cinnamon. Spread mixture evenly in the pan. Place well-drained apricots and cherries over the sugar mixture.

Sift together flour, baking powder, and salt. Beat egg yolks in a bowl. Slowly add sugar and continue beating until yolks are thick. Add hot water and flour mixture to yolks and blend well.

Beat egg whites until stiff. Fold into flour-yolk mixture and spread over the fruit.

Bake 35 minutes or until cake tester comes out clean. Cool on a rack 15 minutes.

Run a knife around the edges and place serving plate over pan, invert and turn out carefully onto plate. Cool completely and serve.

If you wish, sprinkle the powdered sugar on top. (But that will add calories.)

*NOTE: Vanilla sugar: Place 2 cups powdered sugar into a container with a tight cover. Add 1 vanilla bean, cover, and let stand for 3 days.

GRANITA AL CAFFÈ *Coffee Ice*

serves 6

2 cups water
½ cup sugar
4 cups expresso coffee
(or regular strong coffee)
Sweetened whipped cream
(optional)
Grated chocolate or nutmeg

In a saucepan bring water and sugar to boil, stirring constantly. Reduce heat and simmer 7 minutes. Remove from heat and cool to room temperature.

Add coffee, then pour into an ice tray. Freeze for 3 hours. Every 20–25 minutes stir the coffee, scraping the frosty particles from the edges of the tray. The texture of the granita should resemble shaved ice.

Fill 6 wine glasses ¾ full with the coffee ice. If you wish, top with whipped cream. Sprinkle with chocolate or nutmeg, right onto the coffee or on top of the whipped cream.

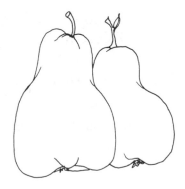

about 3½ cups

GRANITA AL MANDARINO

Tangerine Ice

2 Tbs honey
*2½ cups tangerine juice
(juice of 12 medium
tangerines), strained
*1 tsp finely grated
tangerine peel
3 Tbs tangerine or
orange liqueur
Garnish: tangerine sections

Mix honey with 3 tablespoons of tangerine juice in a bowl. Add remaining tangerine juice, tangerine peel, and liqueur. Pour mixture into an 8″ × 12″ × 2½″ china or glass serving dish and freeze, covered, for about 3 hours without stirring.

Before serving, break up surface with a fork. Stir gently. If it is not soft enough to stir, soften in the refrigerator.

Serve garnished with tangerine sections.

*NOTE: Orange juice and peel may be used instead of tangerine.

about 4 cups

GRANITA AL MELLONE

Watermelon Ice

1 cup water
⅔ cup sugar
*3½ cups watermelon puree

Cook water and sugar in a saucepan over low heat, stirring constantly, until sugar dissolves. Bring to boil without stirring. Reduce heat and simmer uncovered for 6 minutes. Cool and refrigerate for about 3 hours.

Strain the watermelon puree into a bowl. Add cold sugar syrup to the puree. Pour into a nonbreakable glass bowl. Freeze, covered, for 1–1½ hours.

Beat with an electric beater until smooth. Freeze another 1–1½ hours and beat again. Freeze for about 2 more hours until almost solid.

Serve in champagne glasses. The *granita* should be semisoft.

*NOTE: Cut watermelon into small cubes and purée in a blender.

INDEX

Fish and seafood (*cont.*)
　41; trout with mushrooms, 75 (*See also* Shellfish)
Flavorings (*See* Herbs, spices, and flavorings)
Fontina cheese and red pepper antipasto, 28–29
Fresh lima bean soup, 43
Fresh pasta dough, 132
Fresh tomato soup, 42
Frittata (*See* Eggs)
Fritters, two-color, 137
Frothy omelet, 68–69
Fruits (*See under names of*)
Funghi (*See* Mushrooms)

Garden antipasto, 32
Garden sauce, 113
Genoese fish stew, 75
Genoese sea bass, 76
Granita (*See* Ices)
Green beans: with chervil, 59; purée of, 61
Green peppers, stuffed, 98 (*See also* Peppers)
Green ravioli with cheese, 126

Ham (*See* Prosciutto)
Hearty omelet with leeks, 66
Herbs, spices, and flavorings, 13–14
Homemade pizza, 134–135
Homestyle minestrone, 40

Ices: coffee, 147; tangerine, 148; watermelon, 148
Insalata (*See* Salads)
Italian green salad, 51

Lamb: alla Montecatini, 104–105; with sweet peppers, 104
Lean cassata, 141
Leeks, hearty omelet with, 66
Lemon: mousse, 142; sauce, 111
Ligurian salad, 52
Lima bean soup, fresh, 43
Linguine, tomato and basil sauce for, 110
Lobster sauce, red, 113

Maiale (*See* Pork)
Manicotti Florentine, 128–129
Marinara sauce, 114
Meat (*See under names of*)
Melon mélange, 144
Milk, pork cooked in, 100
Minestrone, homestyle, 40
Mixed vegetable salad, 50

Mousse: cardinale, 143; lemon, 142
Mushrooms: and artichoke salad, 51; filled with fish roe, 34; rice with, 136; soup, 39, 41; stuffed, 30–31; trout with, 75; Verona-style, 56
Mussels: in rice and seafood, 79; soup, 43; and tomato sauce, vermicelli with, 124–125; in vermouth, 80

Neapolitan sauce, 116
Neapolitan tomato sauce, 114
Noodles: fine, and mushroom soup, 39; Florentine, 123

Omelets (*See* Eggs)
Orange(s): custard with mandarin, 143; zabaglione, 141

Pasta: cooking method, 17–18; dough, fresh, 132; filled roll, 121; with fresh tomatoes and herbs, 125; green, 127; green ravioli with cheese, 126; for ravioli, raviolini, agnolotti, and tortellini, 130–131; red, 128; soft, 122; spinach dumplings, 129; Tuscan green, 127; types of, 16–17, 18–20 (*See also* Crepes; Noodles; Vermicelli; etc.)
Peaches: brandied, 145; fluff, 145; stuffed baked, 144
Pears: poached, 146; stuffed, 146
Peas, braised, with prosciutto, 58
Peperonata (*See* Peppers)
Peperoni (*See* Peppers)
Peppers: stuffed, 36; with tomatoes and onions, 33; sweet, 30, 32–33, 104 (*See also* Green peppers; Red peppers)
Pesce (*See* Fish)
Pesto Genoa style, 122–123
Pizza, homemade, 134–135
Poached fish, 76
Poached pears, 146
Polenta (*See* Cornmeal)
Pollo (*See* Chicken)
Pork: chops, with fennel, 99; cooked in milk, 100; on a skewer, 99
Poultry (*See* Capon; Chicken; Duck; Turkey)
Prosciutto: braised peas with, 58; cantaloupe and, 34; and pork on a skewer, 99; soup, 44
Purée of carrots, 60
Purée of green beans, 61

Ravioli: fillings for, 131; green, with cheese, 126; pasta for, 130–131; spinach dumplings, 129

MARINA POLVAY is an internationally-known cuisine consultant, food stylist, radio and television personality, writer, lecturer, teacher of gourmet cooking, and author of several best-selling cookbooks. She travels extensively, teaching and learning more about cooking from all over the world. Her many articles have appeared in such magazines as *Bon Appetit, Cuisine, Town and Country, Gourmet, Tropic, Travel Holiday,* and *Palm Beach Life.*